TWAYNE'S FILMMAKERS SERIES

Frank Beaver, Editor

ALAN RUDOLPH

Alan Rudolph

ALAN RUDOLPH
Romance and a Crazed World

Richard Ness

TWAYNE PUBLISHERS
An Imprint of Simon & Schuster Macmillan
New York
PRENTICE HALL INTERNATIONAL
London • Mexico City • New Delhi • Singapore • Sydney • Toronto

Twayne's Filmmakers Series

Alan Rudolph: Romance and a Crazed World
Richard Ness

Twayne Publishers
An Imprint of Simon & Schuster Macmillan
1633 Broadway
New York, NY 10019

Library of Congress Cataloging-in-Publication Data
Ness, Richard.
    Alan Rudolph / Richard Ness.
        p.   cm.   —(Twayne's filmmakers series)
    Filmography: p.
    Includes bibliographical references and index.
    ISBN 0-8057-7847-0 (hardcover). — ISBN 0-8057-9247-3 (paper)
    1. Rudolph, Alan—Criticism and interpretation. I. Title.
    II. Series.
    PN1998.3.R84N47   1996
    791.43'0233'092—dc20   96-27579
                                                                                    CIP

10 9 8 7 6 5 4 3 2 1 (hc)
10 9 8 7 6 5 4 3 2 1 (pb)

Printed in the United States of America.

For Karen
Because she has seen more of these films
than anyone else I know
And because I owe her

CONTENTS

FOREWORD

Of all the contemporary arts, the motion picture is particularly timely and diverse as a popular culture enterprise. This lively art form cleverly combines storytelling with photography to achieve what has been a quintessential twentieth-century phenomenon. Individual as well as national and cultural interests have made the medium an unusually varied one for artistic expression and analysis. Films have been exploited for commercial gain, for political purposes, for experimentation, and for self-exploration. The various responses to the motion picture have given rise to different labels for both the fun and the seriousness with which this art form has been received, ranging from "the movies" to "cinema." These labels hint at both the theoretical and sociological parameters of the film medium.

A collective art, the motion picture has nevertheless allowed individual genius to flourish in all its artistic and technical areas: directing, screenwriting, cinematography, acting, editing. The medium also encompasses many genres beyond the narrative film, including documentary, animated, and avant-garde expression. The range and diversity of motion pictures suggest rich opportunities for appreciation and for study.

Twayne's Filmmakers Series examines the full panorama of motion picture history and art. Many studies are auteur-oriented and elucidate the work of individual directors whose ideas and cinematic styles make them the authors of their films. Other studies examine film movements and genres or analyze cinema from a national perspective. The series seeks to illuminate all the many aspects of film for the film student, the scholar, and the general reader.

Frank Beaver

PREFACE

> Philosophers will naturally assume that it is one thing, and quite clear how, to let a philosophical work teach you how to consider it, and another thing, and quite obscure how or why, to let a film teach you this. I believe these are not such different things.
>
> —Stanley Cavell, *Pursuits of Happiness* (1981)

> Yeah, well you can't live on philosophy.
>
> —Hawk (Kris Kristofferson) in *Trouble in Mind* (1986)

The style is immediately recognizable. A restless, prowling camera follows characters moving in slow motion, as if in a dream, accompanied by the bluesy sound of muted horns. This is the cinematic universe of Alan Rudolph.

Perhaps among American directors only Woody Allen has a style that can be so readily identified from the opening shots of a film. Although he has received less critical attention than many of his contemporaries, Rudolph, in his most personal works, has developed a unique cinematic style and created a self-contained universe peopled by artists and con artists, believers and deceivers. Drawing on established film formulas, Rudolph has combined these cinematic codes with a modern (even postmodern) sensibility. His most characteristic works provide an odd mixture of romantic pursuits and more dangerous conflicts, as though the protagonists of a vintage screwball comedy have become trapped in the environment of the film noir. Rudolph may seem consciously nostalgic in incorporating these genre aspects in his work, but he remains defiantly contemporary in the attitudes, desires, and pursuits of his characters. The films suggest a modern environment in which romance is still desired but is complicated by violence, paranoia, and deception.

Since the 1977 release of *Welcome to L.A.*, his first major work, Rudolph has received divided critical assessments. Some have objected to what they consider self-consciously arty effects, while others admire Rudolph's stylistic experiments and defiance of traditional narrative construction. Even one of his most acclaimed works, *Choose Me* (1984), met with opposition from some critics, most notably Rex Reed, whose *New York Post* review called the film "an absolute pre-requisite for anyone who feels a burning desire to learn how to make bad movies," and added that the director had no discernible talent.[1] Two years earlier, in the same publication, Reed had given a generally positive review to Rudolph's less personal production, *Endangered Species* (1982). Reviews of Rudolph's *The Moderns* (1988) were also greatly divided, with some critics regarding it as one of the best films of the year and others, particularly Vincent Canby of the *New York Times,* considering it amateurish. To date, Rudolph has not made a film which has been unanimously praised or condemned. Yet the vehemence with which he has attracted both defenders and detractors in itself justifies a closer examination of his work.

One reason for the lack of serious attention to Rudolph's work may be that critics have tended to divide his films into those conceived by the director and those generated by studios (a distinction that Rudolph himself has encouraged in interviews). Early films, such as *Welcome to L.A.* and *Remember My Name* (1978), were small, independent works that showed the emergence of a personal style. The lack of financial success, however, forced Rudolph to temporarily abandon his own projects (including *The Moderns,* a film he planned to make after *Welcome to L.A.* but would not be able to do until 1988) in order to work on studio-generated productions. Following his return to independent filmmaking with *Choose Me,* Rudolph summed up his studio experiences in an article in *Film Comment:* "I've learned that when I try to mold what I'm thinking into what other people want, it doesn't work. Bastards come out. I've spent my whole life basically going in the wrong direction on the freeway. I'm definitely out of step with the masses, but that's not to say they can't respond to what I do. My movies aren't *that* esoteric."[2]

Despite his expressed frustrations with the studio system, Rudolph has continued to alternate between working on his own projects and working for others, and as his distinctive directorial style has developed, it has carried over into those projects that Rudolph considers to be less personal. As evidence, one need only observe the initial appearance of Demi Moore in the opening of the 1991 film *Mortal Thoughts,* a work which Rudolph took over after production had begun. From Moore's first entrance, moving in slow motion and accompanied by Mark Isham's ethereal score, the viewer has entered a world that is uniquely Rudolph's. While the studio-generated projects often take place in definable locales (Colorado in *Endangered Species,* the various cities in *Roadie* [1980] or the blue-collar New Jersey neighborhoods of *Mortal Thoughts*), even these are transformed in such a way as to become part of Rudolph's personal geography.

Another potential factor in the lack of recognition of Rudolph's own style has been the inevitable comparisons to his mentor, Robert Altman. While their association has been limited to Rudolph working in various capacities on a handful of Altman's films and Altman serving as producer for three of Rudolph's films (most recently, after a 15-year gap, on *Mrs. Parker and the Vicious Circle* [1994]), the connection was so firmly established at the beginning of Rudolph's directorial career that it has often resulted in his own vision and style being overlooked or misinterpreted by those too willing to identify him simply as an Altman imitator. Even less recognized has been the influence Rudolph has had on Altman's later work. As this study will indicate, their relationship is less of mentor and student than that of two artists who have mutually influenced each other.

Just as Rudolph modifies locations to conform to his own vision, so does he transform genre formulas to match his principal concerns. Whereas many directors have been able to establish a personal voice by focusing their most characteristic work within a specific genre (Alfred Hitchcock with the suspense thriller or John Ford with the western are obvious examples), Rudolph, like Altman, has adapted a number of genres to his thematic interests. Even works where the genre territory seems familiar at the outset have a way of veering off into an environment that is unique to the director. Whether drawing on conventions of women's melodramas (*Remember My Name*), film noir (*Trouble in Mind*), westerns (*Songwriter* [1985]), political thrillers (*Endangered Species*), detective films (*Love at Large* [1989]), suspense dramas (*Mortal Thoughts*) or comedies, both romantic (*Choose Me*) and slapstick (*Roadie*), Rudolph's primary concern in these formulaic situations remains with the interactions of the people rather than in the situations themselves.

This book grew out of a study of *Choose Me* in relation to the work of Stanley Cavell. In *Pursuits of Happiness* Cavell identifies a genre of Hollywood films he has labeled the "remarriage comedy." Cavell regards the genre as a variation of the structure of Shakespearean romantic comedy, in which a young couple has to overcome individual and social obstacles before they can be united in marriage. The remarriage genre defined by Cavell presents a couple already married (or who at least share some past relationship), and the narrative drive does not involve getting the couple together but getting them *back* together. Cavell identifies several characteristics of the genre, including the use of disguises and deceptions, a shared language between the two lovers, and the presence of a "green world" to which the couple retreats to sort out their problems. In analyzing seven films, Cavell observed potential melodramatic elements that threatened the inevitable reconciliation of the couple, and subsequently he established a second genre, "the melodrama of the unknown woman." In these films, as Cavell states, the heroine "will not find herself in what the comedies teach us marriage is, but accordingly in something less or conceivably more than that."[3]

In examining Rudolph in the context of Cavell's work, I have discerned elements of both genres in his films. While the relationship of Mickey and Eve in *Choose Me* contains a number of the elements of remarriage comedy, the character of Nancy Love seems more readily reflective of the melodrama of the unknown woman. Although Cavell's ideas will to some degree inform these readings of Rudolph's films, this study is less interested in the specifics of Cavell's theories (Rudolph, for example, makes little use of the role of maternal figures, which Cavell considers an essential component of the melodrama of the unknown woman) than in using some of his general concepts as a springboard for examining themes and issues in Rudolph's work, particularly in regard to his female characters. Rudolph's combining of elements from Cavell's two genres—not only in *Choose Me* but in a number of his films—suggests that in contemporary society marriage and romantic commitment are still potential goals but that characters also seek to define themselves on a private level outside of their relationships with others.

Because this is the first book-length study of Rudolph's work, its primary goal is to identify and analyze the basic motifs and themes of the films, as well as the stylistic elements that characterize Rudolph's oeuvre. One of the difficulties in writing about Rudolph's films is that they depend on an establishment of mood that is hard to capture in the written word, particularly because a major component in creating that atmosphere is music. As with the work of the painters Rudolph's visual style often emulates, any attempt to translate into words what has been presented can never do complete justice to the experience of viewing the film. Another difficulty in dealing with the films is that the various interactions and multiple relationships that occur in many of the films can sound confusing in a written synopsis, despite the clarity with which they are presented on screen. Therefore, the discussion of each film attempts to provide at the outset a general thematic outline and introduction to the major characters rather than a complete plot synopsis.

In keeping with Rudolph's own evaluation of his work and the response of most critics, I have divided the films into personal and studio-generated works. Rather than follow a strict chronology, I have devoted the first section to individual chapters on Rudolph's more personal works. This is followed by an extended section analyzing his "director-for-hire" projects. Rudolph's most recent film, *Mrs. Parker and the Vicious Circle,* is discussed in the last chapter, as it in many ways combines aspects of his personal and studio-generated projects.

A number of people deserve recognition for their contributions in the completion of this text. A special thanks to Kevin Klimowski and Jenifer Mercer-Klimowski, Jim Lang, Karen Irvin (especially for locating *Premonition*), Lynne Carey and Navid Emami, Tom and Joy Macy, Alissa Simon of the Film Center of Chicago, and Vincent Nebride of Fine Line Features for providing access to materials. The suggestions and encouragement of Charles L. Silet and Leland Poague at Iowa State University were greatly appreciated, as was the assistance of Don Sprague and the computer expertise of Dave Touney. Finally, a thank you to Rebecca Morton and to David Blocker and Sandra Tomita at RainCity for returning my phone calls and answering even my most obscure questions. And, as always, to my parents, Rose and Dick Ness, for their continuing encouragement and support.

CHRONOLOGY

1943	Alan Rudolph born 18 December, the son of actor/director Oscar Rudolph.
1954	Appears in cameo role in film *The Rocket Man*, directed by his father.
1967	Enters Directors Guild Training Program.
1967–1973	Works as assistant director on numerous theatrical films, television programs, and made-for-television movies.
1970	Directs *Premonition* (released in 1972).
1973	Directs *Terror Circus* (also released as *Barn of the Naked Dead* and *Nightmare Circus*); works as assistant director on Robert Altman's *The Long Goodbye*, which begins his association with the director.
1974	*California Split* (assistant director).
1975	*Nashville* (assistant director); *Welcome to My Nightmare* (script for television production).
1976	*Buffalo Bill and the Indians, or Sitting Bull's History Lesson* (co-writer; winner of the Best Film prize at the Berlin Film Festival; voted one of the Ten Best Films of the Year by *Time* magazine).
1977	*Welcome to L.A.*
1978	*Remember My Name* (Geraldine Chaplin is awarded a best actress prize at the Paris Film Festival).
1980	*Roadie.*
1982	*Endangered Species.*
1983	*Return Engagement.*
1984	*Choose Me.* (Rudolph is awarded New Generation Prize by the Los Angeles Film Critics)

1985   *Songwriter* (receives an Academy Award nomination for Song Score Adaptation).

1986   *Trouble in Mind* (winner of Independent Spirit Award for Best Cinematography; awarded a Jussi [Finland] Diploma for Foreign Film).

1987   *Made in Heaven.*

1988   *The Moderns* (awarded a Jussi Diploma for Foreign Film).

1989   *Love at Large.*

1991   *Mortal Thoughts.*

1992   Rudolph makes a cameo appearance in Altman's *The Player.*

1993   *Equinox.*

1994   *Mrs. Parker and the Vicious Circle.*

INTRODUCTION: DEFINING THE RUDOLPH UNIVERSE

Truly fertile Music, the only kind that will move us, that we shall truly appreciate, will be a Music conducive to Dream, which banishes all reason and analysis. One must not wish first to understand and then to feel. Art does not tolerate Reason.

—Albert Camus, "Essay on Music" (1932)

Reality is a question of perspective; the further you get from the past, the more concrete and plausible it seems—but as you approach the present, it inevitably seems incredible.

—Salman Rushdie, "All-India Radio" (1981)

There is a decisive (and divisive) moment in Alan Rudolph's *Choose Me* (1984) that determines how audiences respond to the director's filmmaking style. The film concerns two women—Eve (Lesley Ann Warren) and Nancy (Genevieve Bujold)—who have become roommates and have both become involved with the enigmatic Mickey (Keith Carradine). Nancy is a radio sex therapist and Eve is one of her frequent callers (although the roommates are not aware that each is the voice on the other end of the phone). In a key scene, Mickey has had a sexual liaison with Nancy, and he has also asked Eve to marry him. Eve calls into Nancy's radio program and the two women talk, neither aware of the other's identity and also unaware that they are discussing the same man. The camera pans with Eve as she crosses the room, carrying the phone while she talks. As she crosses back, Nancy suddenly appears behind her, echoing Eve's words about "the thrill" of a relationship. When Eve crosses back again, Nancy is gone.

In this scene Rudolph deliberately contradicts the viewer's expectations of screen space. The location of each character has been clearly defined, and Nancy's abrupt appearance in Eve's house defies that logic. The moment is not intended to be taken literally, yet it is also too deliberate to be ignored. By suddenly projecting Nancy into Eve's personal space, Rudolph visually depicts a telepathic connection between the two women and calls attention to the artificial nature of cinematic reality. The shot becomes an attempt to reach an understanding of these characters that goes beyond their physical presence and what can be revealed through dialogue into a presentation of their psychological states.

Rudolph has said that the scene is either people's favorite or least favorite moment in the film, and he seems to enjoy that ambiguity. Throughout his films there are such moments that defy cinematic convention. Characters will seem to share the same dream or one will suddenly be projected into a scene in response to the thoughts of another. In his later work Rudolph has extended the unrealistic elements to the environment itself, with the external world at times presented in a deliberately stylized and artificial manner.

Rudolph's incorporation of such elements is more a contradiction of cinematic convention than one of reality. The director has said that he does not make realistic movies because movies themselves are a lie on reality.[1] His defiance of the "rules" of screen space and narrative construction actually enhance rather than defy reality by making the characters' psychological reality as much a part of the visual presentation as their physical reality. He is able to translate into visual and aural terms not just what his characters do but also what they feel: "It seems as if our emotional connection, the things we don't understand, are [sic] much more real and accurate, more representative of the purpose of life, than anything tangible."[2]

If there is a dynamic in Rudolph's most characteristic work it is the conflict between real and processed emotion. His characters exist in an environment where romanticism in various forms has been packaged and sold, so that these individuals find themselves seeking an image of romance rather than responding to their instinctive feelings. They analyze relationships and seek assurance from the artifices of popular culture that permeate modern society. Rudolph also incorporates violence as an aspect of this environment—an aspect that seems to act as an obstacle to romantic fulfillment. Yet violence itself (particularly when associated with the movies of the past) has been processed as a kind of romanticism. The real villains in Rudolph's films are those who have packaged emotion (whether violent, passionate, or both) for profit. Progressively in Rudolph's work, this translates into a confrontation between corruption and innocence.

To reconcile true emotions with the artificial images of emotion with which they are surrounded, Rudolph's characters often resort to deception. In the opening scene of *Welcome to L.A.* (1977), Karen (Geraldine Chaplin), who fancies herself the heroine of a Garbo film and continually repeats phrases cribbed from Goya and others, makes the personal observation that "people deceive themselves here. . . . And that's how they fall in love." Her observation establishes a major concern of the director up through his most recent film, *Mrs. Parker and the Vicious Circle* (1994). It is in working through the deceptions that Rudolph's characters and his films take on their fascination.

The director's multicharacter constructions, in which the lives of a number of individuals intersect by chance or coincidence, are an obvious link to Rudolph's association with Robert Altman, but Rudolph tends to focus on groups of interactions within these broad canvases. In an interview in *Revue du Cinéma,* Rudolph stated his belief that the triangle is the basic, natural state of modern relationships.[3] His films, however, defy geometric constructions (as well as basic film formulas) by establishing a multiplicity of triangles within a single film, many of which share a common apex. Adding to the complexity of the structure, these triangles do not always involve three individuals. In some cases the hypotenuse is created by outside, nonhuman forces that cause complications for the couple. Thus, for example, in *Welcome to L.A.,* the marriage of Harvey Keitel and Geraldine Chaplin already has a triangular configuaration, as Keitel appears to be devoted as much to his career as to his family, even before one is aware of his outside relationship with Sissy Spacek or Chaplin's later interaction with Keith Carradine. This latter relationship takes the form of a more traditional romantic triangle, with Carradine, Chaplin, and Keitel as the three components, although Carradine also serves as one side of a number of other triangles involving the film's various characters.

As well as being multicharacter, Rudolph's worlds are multicultural. From his first directorial effort, the low-budget horror film *Premonition* (1970), Rudolph has introduced characters of various ethnic and cultural backgrounds into his films. Unlike most Hollywood productions, the director does not incorporate these performers to call deliberate attention to racial distinctions. But neither does he deny them their ethnicity—a charge that has often been leveled against more mainstream films. In Rudolph's most personal projects he presents urban environments that have become a melting pot of diverse cultures and ideologies and that seem to exist in no definable time or place. Significantly, the studio-generated projects on which he has worked have shown a good deal less cultural diversity.

The multiplicity of cultures suggests the potential for a range of languages, and Rudolph uses language as an indication of both unification and isolation. His protagonists often speak in a kind of heightened language that adds to the feeling that they do not exist in any identifiable time or place. Language becomes a factor in defining character, as demonstrated, for example, by the repeated quotations (and misquotations) of Karen in *Welcome to L.A.* Mutually understood language becomes a means of uniting characters and also serves to isolate them from others. At other times misunderstanding creates separation, as characters talk at cross-purposes. Rudolph often uses these misunderstandings for comic effect. The complexities of *Choose Me,* for example, culminate in a convoluted conversation between Keith Carradine and Lesley Ann Warren in a car in which each believes the other is talking about something else. Those individuals who understand one another's language have the greatest potential for romantic fulfillment—a concept that reinforces the connection to Cavell's genre of remarriage. In addition, a number of Rudolph's female characters establish their status as unknown women by speaking of themselves in the third person (Nancy in *Choose Me* and Beverly in *Equinox* [1993], for example), suggesting that their unknowingness extends even to themselves.

Adding to the sense of heightened language is Rudolph's use of poet characters who at times become directly involved in the various interactions but are also able to comment on the events from a distance. This concept is established as early as *Welcome to L.A.,* with Carroll Barber's songs serving as commentary on the various relationships, many of which directly involve him. Like Carroll, Pearl in *Choose Me* and Solo in *Trouble in Mind* (1986) create their own poetry and hover on the periphery of the main action while reciting it. Particularly in Solo's case, his poetic recitations seem not only to be commenting on events but also to some degree controlling them, and this concept becomes more pronounced in Rudolph's later works. *The Moderns* (1988) uses the historical figure of Ernest Hemingway as a peripheral character who seems to be mentally recording the events he witnesses presumably with the intention of making the participants in these events the principal characters of his own work. One could also interpret, however, that these individuals and incidents are a product of his creation rather than a source of inspiration. This further level of complexity also surfaces in *Equinox*. In addition to Beverly, who performs the familiar role of commentator by occasionally reciting Emily Dickinson poems in voice-over to comment on events, Rudolph employs the character of Sonya, a short story writer who may be creating what we see on screen. In *Mrs. Parker and the Vicious Circle* Rudolph once again employs an actual writer, and while she is the major character she is also seen at periodic points in isolated black-and-white shots as she recites her poems, which provide an additional dimension to the events being depicted.

Along with poets, Rudolph makes frequent use of artists and musicians. These characters not only act as commentators but must also deal with issues of artistic integrity in a commercialized society. The conflict between commercialization and artistry has become a progressive concern in the director's work. *Welcome to L.A.* ends with Carroll's decision to record his own music, and the gesture reflects his need to establish some sense of his own identity. While the individuals involved in shaping Carroll's career do not appear to be acting out of exploitative motives, Rudolph's later films would establish a financially based power structure in which art is exploited by those in power, as demonstrated by Hilly Blue in *Trouble in Mind* and Bertram Stone in *The Moderns*. The latter film provides the most extended meditation on how art itself is defined and merchandised.

Rudolph also creates a specific atmosphere through visual devices. Adding to the dreamlike quality of his films is the use of slow motion and a constantly moving camera. Rudolph has suggested that the latter technique grew out of necessity, because the limited budgets and shooting schedules for his films allowed less time for multiple coverage of a scene (Smith, 61). Nevertheless, the restless camera is an appropriate visual counterpart to his characters' continual quest for identity. The camera also contributes to the characters' unknown qualities, with tracking shots often moving into tight close-ups, as though trying to penetrate a person's innermost thoughts. The mobile camera has resulted in progressively longer takes in Rudolph's films, with some shots in *The Moderns* and *Mrs. Parker* running several minutes. In addition to generating a fluid quality, this technique allows the performers to develop a scene in greater detail and preserve the integrity of their interactions. Even in these long takes, Rudolph makes careful use of compositions to define relationships between characters. A favorite stylistic device, evident as early as *Premonition,* involves a zoom from a two-shot to a close-up of one of the characters, creating a feeling of intimacy but also of isolation. Rudolph also employs mirror shots to visually reinforce the characters' search for identity, as well as to call attention to the distinction between image and reality.

As Rudolph's films have become reflective of the power structures in society, they have also become more aware of the potential for redemption. In general, his films either end with the protagonists achieving some form of romantic fulfillment (*Choose Me, Songwriter, Love at Large*) or seeking to escape from an oppressive environment (*Remember My Name, Trouble in Mind, Equinox*), either in the form of a literal departure or a retreat into self-deception and isolation from the outside world. As Rudolph's vision of urban decay has become darker, these escapes have become associated with the concept of spiritual redemption. Hawk's escape from the exploitative environment of Rain City in *Trouble in Mind,* for example, is accompanied by a momentary vision of the angelic Georgia, the film's symbol of innocence. Spiritual redemption is a major theme of *Made in Heaven* (1987) and carries over to Stone's resurrection in *The Moderns* and to the spiritual elements of *Equinox.*

In *Equinox* redemption becomes equated with the search for self. This has been a concern of Rudolph's protagonists since the self-reflexive address to the camera by Karen that begins *Welcome to L.A.* (and that actually has its origins even earlier in Neil's first-person commentary in *Premonition).* These characters are seeking some personal truth, but, as the director himself has indicated, "emotional truth is a rather fragile concept. Objective reality seems even more distant to me. Fact, time and subjectivity tend to be an uneasy alliance. Add romance and a crazed world, and truth becomes downright negotiable."[4] Throughout his career, Rudolph has continued to redefine both truth and reality in terms of his personal worldview. Yet for all the chaos and coincidence that seems to erupt in this world, the director, like his characters, continues to search for ways to make sense of it. From *Welcome to L.A.*'s Karen, who attempts to unravel the mysteries of love from the back seat of a taxi cab, to the title character of *Mrs. Parker and the Vicious Circle,* who also directly addresses the viewer as the film opens, Rudolph's romantics continue to seek, and invite the viewer to search for, understanding. As the director stated in another interview, "I think each new film is going to be a new beginning. But they all turn out to be about the same thing."[5]

CHAPTER I

Early Years: The Altman Connection

In twenty years, Alan will be considered among the great filmmakers of his time. In the meantime, he'll just keep making movies like he's doing now.
　　　　　—Robert Altman, quoted in *American Film* (March 1986)

Alan Rudolph's choice of career and appreciation of past Hollywood traditions are not surprising, given his upbringing. His father, Oscar, had been a child actor in Hollywood in the 1930s and later became a film and television director. Among his directorial credits are *Twist Around the Clock* (1961) and *Don't Knock the Twist* (1962), which, in their own way, anticipate the potential combining of music and visuals that would find greater expression in his son's work. While many of his contemporaries learned their craft in film school, Rudolph was able to get a firsthand view of the industry as a child growing up in Los Angeles. He even made a cameo appearance in one of his father's productions, *The Rocket Man* (1954). The fantasy, co-scripted by Lenny Bruce, involved a small boy who gets hold of a gun that turns crooked people honest.[1] This close Hollywood connection might seem ironic for a director whose films have often been described as being closer to European art films than mainstream American productions. But Rudolph's work has continually demonstrated an appreciation of, if not an adherence to, traditional Hollywood formulas.

　　The elder Rudolph's extensive television work provided his son with entry into the business and an appreciation for working on tight schedules and limited budgets. Although Rudolph briefly attended UCLA, where he majored in accounting, he soon turned his attention to making short films (often for friends who were enrolled in film school) and got a job in the mail room at Paramount. In 1967 he entered the training program of the Directors Guild of America and became one of the youngest assistant directors in Hollywood. Rudolph worked as an assistant on various television programs in the late 1960s and early 1970s, including many directed by his father, while pursuing feature film work. Despite the wide range of projects on which he worked, however, Rudolph does not receive screen credit on many of the films for which he was an assistant director, and the exact nature of his contributions is difficult to determine. Among the more notable films in which he was involved were *Marooned* (1969), *The Traveling Executioner* (a 1970 release that co-starred Bud Cort, already a member of Robert Altman's stock company), and *The Arrangement* (1969). His work as assistant director on Buzz Kulik's *Riot* (1969) may have influenced his later use of characters with prison backgrounds in both *Remember My Name* and *Trouble in Mind*. In an interview in *Revue du Cinéma,* Rudolph stated that "the action of leaving prison and starting anew is one of the great metaphors in life" (Garel, 79).

Rudolph claims that while working as an assistant director he became disillusioned with the mistakes being made by crews and the mediocre material being produced. The break from his career as an assistant director came while working on a television movie. Rudolph suggested to the director that he not make compromises just to satisfy a tight schedule, and the director then accused him of trying to undermine his work (Smith, 67). After deciding that he did not want to continue in this capacity, Rudolph began to focus on writing his own scripts. He had turned down opportunities to work on *The Great White Hope* (1970) and *The Poseidon Adventure* (1972) when he received a call offering him a job on *The Long Goodbye* (1973). The director was Robert Altman. Although Rudolph was reluctant to take another assistant director job, he went to see Altman's most recent film, *McCabe and Mrs. Miller* (1972), and claims the film was a major influence "because it did what I was really interested in most—create a mood."[2] He immediately signed on to become part of Altman's crew. It would be inappropriate to deny or downplay the importance of Altman as an influential force in Rudolph's development as a filmmaker. It would be equally inaccurate, however, to suggest that Rudolph simply became an imitator of Altman. Rather, the collaboration enabled Rudolph to define and refine his personal vision. It also provided him with an understanding of how one could work within the system without making artistic compromises.

In addition to *The Long Goodbye,* Rudolph apprenticed with Altman on *California Split* (1974) and *Nashville* (1975) and co-scripted *Buffalo Bill and the Indians, or Sitting Bull's History Lesson* (1976) with the director. Of these, the latter two films are most often cited as influencing the Rudolph style, especially when viewed as a progression toward *Welcome to L.A.* The earlier films also provide intriguing connections to Rudolph's later work. The laconic gumshoe of *The Long Goodbye* could easily be a forerunner of one of Rudolph's displaced romantics (particularly detective Harry Dobbs in *Love at Large*). *The Long Goodbye*'s incorporation of film noir conventions that do not seem to work out quite the same when placed in the context of contemporary egocentric Hollywood society is a theme that Rudolph would take up in his own films. The alienated Southern California milieu of the film would become the setting for *Welcome to L.A.* and would also be an environment to which Altman would return in *The Player* (1992) and *Short Cuts* (1993). Similarly, one can point to *California Split* as providing early indications of the emphasis on commerce in defining success, which will surface in both Rudolph's and Altman's later films. The casinos of *California Split* are obvious forerunners of the Lotto signs that offer the promise of financial security in *Equinox*. One can also find in *California Split* the concept of self-deception that is a defining feature of many of Rudolph's characters.

It is *Nashville,* however, that appears to provide the clearest blueprint for *Welcome to L.A.* This is apparent in the multicharacter structure and the use of the music scene in a defined city as the background. In addition to the general structure, the parallels between the two films are most obvious in the presence of Keith Carradine in both works as a bed-hopping musician who indulges in instant gratifications but seems unable to find personal fulfillment, and Geraldine Chaplin as a character given to reciting vacuous statements while seemingly being unable to connect to the world around her. The humiliation of the character Sueleen (Gwen Welles) when she is forced to strip for a group of men at a club in *Nashville* is echoed in the scene in *Welcome to L.A.* in which Karen (Geraldine Chaplin) appears naked before Carradine in a pathetic gesture of submission to try to elicit some response from him (although it is significant that in *Nashville* the situation demonstrates the victimization of the female character, whereas in Rudolph's film it becomes a part of the process undertaken by Chaplin's character of trying to come to understand and reinvent herself). In both scenes the viewer is not made to share the viewpoint of the male characters but is asked to understand the female character's feelings of humiliation and desperation. Whether the similarities in the two films are due to Rudolph drawing on Altman for inspiration or of Altman incorporating ideas contributed by Rudolph is difficult to determine, although Altman has graciously acknowledged that "a lot of *Nashville* is [Rudolph's] movie" (Rensin, 54). Rudolph allegedly worked, uncredited, on the *Nashville* script, as did many of the principal performers, and it has been suggested that with the film's large cast of characters, Rudolph and the other assistants were often able to create an entire separate story line as part of the background action while Altman concentrated on the elements in the foreground.

More direct credit can be given to Rudolph for the development of *Buffalo Bill and the Indians, or Sitting Bull's History Lesson,* as he and Altman are identified as co-writers. In describing their collaboration at the time of the film's release, Rudolph observed, "Bob sees the light and I dig the tunnel" (Macklin, 2). While the multicharacter structure and self-contained setting are Altman trademarks, elements emerge in the film that have not previously been seen in the director's work, or at least not developed to the extent that they are in *Buffalo Bill.* Disregarding much of the Arthur Kopit play on which the script is allegedly based, Altman and Rudolph provide an exposé on the fradulence of their western "hero" and question how reality can be defined in a society in which truth is repackaged as entertainment. As Rudolph wrote in the script, "Truth is whatever gets the most applause" and "History is nothing more than disrespect for the dead." Buffalo Bill echoes earlier Altman characters, such as Warren Beatty's McCabe or Bud Cort's Brewster McCloud, whose ambitions exceed their abilities, but in this film emphasis is placed not just on the self-deception of the lead character but on the ability to market a deceptive image for mass consumption (the hero is even introduced as just a voice coming from behind a tapestry bearing his image). As such, Buffalo Bill and his Wild West Show represent the commercialization of history and consequently of artistry—a theme to which Rudolph will return in a number of his later works.

Along with depicting a point at which nineteenth-century history became twentieth-century show business, *Buffalo Bill* offers early indications of Rudolph's interest in equating power with control of artistic vision. Early in the film the inhabitants of the camp question why Sitting Bull would be willing to join the Wild West Show, and a journalist responds, "If he wasn't interested in the show business, he wouldn't have become a chief." But in contrast to Bill, who relishes his falsified role as America's national hero, Sitting Bull does not seek audience confirmation of his mythic stature. He has, in fact, only come to the compound because he has been told in dreams that this is where he will meet the great father. The significance of dreams—which will become more pronounced in Rudolph's own films—is used to contrast the two men. The contrast is summed up by the character Ned Buntline's comment that Bill's creation of the Wild West Show is just dreaming out loud. It is also Buntline who identifies the Rudolphian conflict between dreams and reality when he adds that things are starting to take on an unreal shape.

Buntline's premonition becomes most pronounced in the fantasy dream sequence in which Bill is confronted by the ghost of Sitting Bull—an encounter that forces him to face up to his own inadequacies. This scene provides the culmination of Bill's search for his own identity. In anticipation of *Welcome to L.A.* and *Remember My Name,* internal search is reinforced visually through the use of mirror shots. Buntline provides the major challenge to Bill's sense of self, as he takes credit for the creation of Bill's legend, and it is fitting that, when the two men meet, Altman films much of their conversation as a reflection in a mirror. After Buntline toasts Bill with the comment, "It's the thrill of my life to have invented you," and exits, Altman remains on Bill's reflected image, which is half in shadow, implying his own awareness that he is incomplete. Appropriately, Bill is again later filmed in a mirror during the dream sequence, as he chastises his alter ego Buntline for deserting him.

Along with the use of dream imagery, mirror shots, and reflections on commercialization, *Buffalo Bill* demonstrates greater interest in male-female relationships than such earlier Altman works as *M★A★S★H* (1970) and *California Split,* which tended to emphasize male bonding. The brief vignettes in *Buffalo Bill* depicting the relationship between Annie Oakley and Frank Butler (played by Geraldine Chaplin and John Considine, both of whom would figure prominently in destructive relationships in *Welcome to L.A.*), anticipate Rudolph's later work in the intertwining of romance and violence. Buntline can also be seen as an early version of one of Rudolph's poet characters, as he comments on his alleged creation while remaining distanced from the other characters, holding court in a saloon away from the main compound and forcing his creation to come to him. In reviewing *Buffalo Bill and the Indians* for *Film Heritage,* F. Anthony Macklin offered an observation that might have served as a prediction of Rudolph's future work: "The key to the movie is that Altman and his brilliant writer Alan Rudolph are saying that image is not reality. They show that image—what appears to be—is misleading and leads us away from reality. Every line and situation seems to come from this idea."[3]

Altman and Rudolph share an interest in the factors that constitute success in society and the workings of "the show business." Both directors also share an affinity for working variations on traditional Hollywood formulas, but Altman—particularly in his early work—takes a revisionist approach to genre structures, whereas Rudolph's incorporation of such structures in examining the romanticism of his characters reaffirms their basic power. Altman's *The Long Goodbye* deconstructed the detective genre, whereas Rudolph's *Love at Large* reconstructs the genre as a romantic comedy. Altman tends to work from the outside, while Rudolph's films are more introspective. As Rudolph has stated, "We overlap in certain points of view, but our centres are different. Altman nurtures an overview and then fills it in. I seem to begin on details and work out" (Rudolph 1985, 264). Thus, Altman's films often start with a self-contained universe (the compound in *M*A*S*H,* the western town in *McCabe,* the title location in *Nashville,* the Wild West Show in *Buffalo Bill,* the cartoon community in *Popeye* [1980], or even the Houston Astrodome in *Brewster McCloud* [1970]) and then examine who inhabits it. Rudolph, on the other hand, begins with the inhabitants and then works out to examine the environment in which they function. Even in *Welcome to L.A.,* seemingly the most Altmanesque of Rudolph's films, the title location becomes an unrecognizable and anonymous environment that seems to be inhabited only by the characters with which the filmmaker is directly concerned (an approach that elicited numerous criticisms that Rudolph did not even make use of the customary extras in his exterior shots). By contrast, in *Nashville* the city becomes a contributing character and the individuals whose lives are examined exist because, rather than in spite of, its presence.

Summing up his association with Altman at the time of the release of *Welcome to L.A.,* Rudolph observed that "I believe in his vision, and I also have a different vision of my own. I look within, Bob looks without. He has a much broader view of things, he understands the workings of a subject. I get involved in the moment-to-moment emotional range. That's why I'm not really good at plots. My individuals add up to a whole, and Bob's whole gets down to individuals."[4]

While Altman was an important influence on Rudolph's work, it could be argued that the collaboration was equally influential in Altman's later films. In the early 1980s, Altman's work tended to become more streamlined and introspective, with themes that paralleled works being directed by Rudolph. *Fool for Love* (1985), for example, might be viewed as a darker companion to *Choose Me; Vincent and Theo* (1990) shares with *The Moderns* the same concern for the role of commerce in the determination of what constitutes art; and *Short Cuts* can be seen as an updating of *Welcome to L.A.*, with its focus on the interactions of a number of characters in Los Angeles who pursue intertwining relationships and who, significantly, have little or no connection to the town's predominant industry. Although parallels would continue throughout their careers, it would be 15 years before the two would work together again, when Altman produced Rudolph's *Mrs. Parker and the Vicious Circle.* By this time Rudolph's own style and vision had become so established that the film (even with its atmosphere of an Altman-style party) can easily be seen as reflective of the director's themes and concerns.

CHAPTER 2

Welcome to L.A.: Daydreams in Traffic

Is it because acts are not lovely that thou seekest solitude
Where the horrible darkness is impressed with reflections of desire?
— William Blake, "Visions of the Daughters of Albion" (1793)

Rudolph regards the 1977 film *Welcome to L.A.* as his directorial debut, although prior to this he was credited with directing two low-budget horror films, *Premonition* (1970) and *Terror Circus* (1973). The director is reluctant to discuss these films and they are seldom listed among his credits. Rudolph has indicated that these two early experiments were undertaken to get experience as a director, and he contemplated a more serious return to directing during his tenure with Altman. Rudolph first planned to leave after *California Split* but was persuaded to assist on *Nashville* and to co-write *Buffalo Bill and the Indians*. During this time he also prepared scripts for two unrealized Altman projects, *The Yig Epoxy* and the film version of Kurt Vonnegut's *Breakfast of Champions*. As part of the arrangement with the studio on *Buffalo Bill and the Indians*, Altman offered to produce another film for an additional $1 million, which Rudolph would direct.

Welcome to L.A. had its origins during the making of *Nashville*, when composer Richard Baskin played for Rudolph part of a suite of songs he had been working on entitled "City of the One Night Stands." Rudolph decided he could write a script around the songs and eventually Altman took on the project as producer. Rudolph's description of the relationship between composer, director, and producer could easily describe the interactions of the characters in his films: "Richard and I overlap. And Bob and I overlap. Richard and Bob overlap. Sometimes we all overlap. But neither of us is the other person" (Rudolph 1977, 10).

This comment is an indication of the basic structure of the film, in which the lives of several characters overlap briefly during the recording of an album in the title location. This multicharacter structure led to the film being viewed by many critics as an imitation of Altman's films, particularly *Nashville*. The reaction was perhaps inevitable, given Altman's role as producer and the casting of several members of his stock company, most notably Geraldine Chaplin and Keith Carradine, playing what appeared to be extensions of their roles in Altman's study of the country music capital. Nevertheless, *Welcome to L.A.* also offers the first indication of Rudolph's cinematic universe and his emerging visual style.

Rudolph has indicated that the Baskin songs became the plot of the movie and that in a number of places during the editing he removed the dialogue because the music was more eloquent. Like a musical piece, the film is less concerned with a linear plot line and dramatic incident than with the evocation of a mood. What story there is centers on the arrival of composer Carroll Barber (Carradine) to the title location to witness the recording of an album of his material by singer Eric Wood (Richard Baskin). Carroll provides the connecting link to the other characters and becomes involved with nearly every woman he encounters, including his realtor Ann Goode (Sally Kellerman), agent Susan Moore (Viveca Lindfors) and even his father's mistress, Nona Bruce (Lauren Hutton), and secretary, Jeannette Ross (Diahann Abbott). In turn, most of these characters are involved in other relationships, and these are also examined. In keeping with Rudolph's interest in triangular constructions, however, the major interaction in the film involves Carroll, his father's employee Ken Hood (Harvey Keitel), and Ken's neurotic wife, Karen (Chaplin).

The ever-shifting relationships recall the structure of classical comedy, an approach reinforced by the director's use of such terms as *romantic satire* and *absurd fable* in describing it (Rudolph 1985, 264). As such, it would seem to owe something to the elements from which Cavell derived his comedies of remarriage. In assessing what motivates each of these characters and what they learn from their interactions, however, Rudolph acknowledges a desperation and atmosphere of alienation that take the characters beyond the realm of comedy. If Rudolph recognizes the pathetic humor of these individuals, he also shares their pain and loneliness. Each of the characters appears to have come to the film with a good deal of emotional baggage, an impression summed up in one of Baskin's lyrics:

> I've been in love before
> But I got hurt so bad
> That I still can feel the pain
> I want to love again, but I still feel too afraid

It is this fear that has caused many of the characters to shut themselves off from genuine emotions. Some, like Ken and Ann's husband, Jack (John Considine), seek compensation through work or meaningless affairs, while others, such as Karen, substitute the artificial emotions provided by aspects of popular culture.

A distinction between male and female modes of discourse is established at the outset, with the introduction of the Chaplin and

The five female leads appear in this posed publicity shot for *Welcome to L.A.* (1976). From left to right are Karen Hood (Geraldine Chaplin), Nona Bruce (Lauren Hutton), Ann Goode (Sally Kellerman), Susan Moore (Viveca Lindfors), and Linda Murray (Sissy Spacek).
Courtesy Museum of Modern Art/Film Stills Archive.

Carradine characters (the two most closely linked to their earlier *Nashville* roles). Carroll's introduction occurs only in aural terms (he will not appear on screen for several more scenes), as he sings the title song. More than being a conventional theme song, however, the musical piece offers the first indication of Carroll's position as a detached observer, as he will be identified as the writer of the songs that will be used throughout the film to comment on the action. Conflicting with his outsider's viewpoint is the introduction of Karen, who is first seen seated in the back of a cab driving through the deserted streets of the city. She momentarily interrupts the song to directly address the camera/viewer and comment that "people deceive themselves here, don't you think? Yes. And that's how they fall in love. And then when everything is over, it's the other person that gets deceived. . . . I don't need to be loved by anyone. I don't mind waiting. It's how you wait that's important, anyway, I think. But everyone gets deceived. Don't they?" (Her statements echo Lord Henry in Oscar Wilde's *The Picture of Dorian Gray,* who observes, "When one is in love, one always begins by deceiving one's self, and one always ends by deceiving others.")

This opening establishes how these two characters will respond to their various interactions with the others in the film. Befitting his position as the outsider returning to this milieu, Carroll is introduced as an unseen presence. Unlike Karen, whose direct address to the camera suggests a need for reassurance and a desire for a more direct form of communication, Carroll seems to avoid the camera's (and by connection the audience's) scrutiny, and this reflects a more general inability to make a commitment to those with whom he interacts. Yet Karen also remains something of an outside observer and finds it easier to share her feelings with strangers, or even the anonymous audience, than with those to whom she is closest. As will be shown later, her attempts to draw a response from her husband rarely involve direct confrontation, and when they do she resorts to the repetition of phrases taken from others. The introduction of both characters in the opening scene might at first suggest a duality of viewpoint but instead becomes a reflection on how Rudolph's characters will overlap. Even before Karen and Carroll meet, the use of his voice over shots of her in this opening section establishes a connection between them, and Karen's private observations to the camera also introduce the theme of the search for identity that Carroll will eventually have to face. Significantly, only in the film's final shot will he turn to directly acknowledge the camera, as though he has now reached the point at which Karen was in the beginning of the film and has begun his own search for identity.

It is worth noting that this dual introduction calls into question the ongoing critical debate over the role of the camera's gaze in the treatment of male and female characters. In the opening of *Welcome to L.A.* the masculine viewpoint is presented strictly in aural terms, whereas Karen's direct address to the camera (a Brechtian device that is used at various points throughout the film) makes the recording instrument neither voyeuristic observer nor object of revelation but rather a co-conspirator (and a non-gender-specific one) in her philosophical enquiry. The female characters in the film, as in many of Rudolph's later works, will seek some meaning in themselves through their relationships with others, while the male characters try to avoid thinking about or analyzing these interactions. Rudolph will often employ an introspective camera style, but rather than objectifying his characters, the technique contributes to their search to determine their identity.

Rudolph uses both Carroll and Karen, despite their seeming detachment, to introduce us to the remaining characters. In these early scenes the geometric complexity of Rudolph's structure becomes apparent. Even before Carradine arrives, there is a triangularity at work in the relationship of Karen and her husband, Ken, who seems devoted as much to his work as to his family. There is also a suggestion of Ken's extramarital associations, including attempted relationships with the housekeeper Linda (Sissy Spacek) and the real estate agent Ann. Linda, in turn, is already involved in an affair with Ann's husband, Jack. The arrival of Carroll complicates all of these relationships and adds additional geometric configurations. Carroll has an affair with Nona, the mistress of his father, Carl (Denver Pyle), which in turn creates a conflict in Carroll's relationship with his agent Susan. Once Carroll becomes directly involved with these characters, his position as detached observer is taken over by singer Eric Wood, who acts as surrogate by singing the songs Carroll has written.

While all of the other characters seem to be searching for something, Eric is the one character whose goals or sense of identity are never addressed in the film, and he maintains an almost unreal distance from them while providing the circumstance under which their lives intersect. Although his recording studio provides a pivotal location around which much of the action revolves, he remains detached from these characters, and his songs are used (like those of Alan Price in Lindsay Anderson's *O Lucky Man!* [1973]) as a kind of Greek chorus to comment on events. At several points in the film the

songs are heard over shots of Carroll driving, as he moves from conquest to conquest. The musical score generates an overall melancholy
mood for the film, and it occasionally comments on other characters
as well. At one point the lyrics reinforce the theme of a search for
identity, as Susan breaks down in front of a mirror while Baskin on
the soundtrack sings, "I must have met you once before / But lookin'
at you now I ain't so sure." Although Karen initially rejects Carroll
and tells him she is not what he needs, the song lyrics later succinctly
sum up the nature of their relationship, as Rudolph alternates separate shots of the two of them, accompanied by the lyric "You wanna
run but sometimes you just gotta choose / Between what you need
and what you're too damn scared to lose."

Karen would seem to be equated (or at least would equate herself)
with Cavell's concept of the unknown woman in that she seems to
be seeking to define herself in terms of something more than what
she has been able to gain from marriage, and in fact she has come to
recognize marriage as another form of deception. Her relationship
with Ken offers at least the possibility of remarriage, however. But
whereas Cavell specifically identifies the transformation of the female
character as an aspect of the remarriage genre, in Rudolph's film the
"remarriage" takes the form of the alteration of the male character.
By the end of the film the characters have effectively traded positions, with Ken reduced to sitting in a corner, recalling one of the
earliest shots of Karen being photographed by Nona as she hovers in
a stairwell. Following Ken's attempt at reconciliation near the end of
the film, Karen reverts back to the carefully rehearsed lines and quotations she has used throughout the film, which in themselves constitute a form of self-deception. Thus, their relationship is left at the end
somewhere between Cavell's two genres, with the male character
believing in the potential for remarriage by trying to understand the
unknown woman who has emerged during the course of their marital existence.

Rudolph's characters also deviate from Cavell's concepts in their
awareness of their own philosophical development as a result of their
relationships with others. While Cavell's philosophical considerations
largely grow out of his responses to viewing the films rather than
being a concern of the characters within them (Peter and Ellie in
Frank Capra's *It Happened One Night* [1934] are undoubtedly
unaware of the Emersonian resonances they elicit), the characters in
Rudolph's films have been shaped by an increased social emphasis on
psychological, sociological, and philosophical considerations, and consequently such elements have become a part of their conversation.

Karen at times employs philosophical rhetoric as a means of attack, as when she proclaims to her disinterested husband, "The sleep of reason produces monsters," a Goya quote she uses throughout the film (although she initially misattributes it to Benjamin Franklin and has to be corrected by Carroll). In Karen's case, the quote becomes an empty repetition rather than an attempt to understand herself or her world through philosophical inquiry. A more tangible reference point for her is not the observations of Goya but the dialogue of Garbo, more specifically from the film *Camille* (1937). Her identification with the character even takes the form of coughing and trying to convince others that she is dying. Both her funereal and filmic obsesssions tie in with her notions of romanticism, with Garbo providing an important image of the romantic who suffers for love. At one point Karen states, "Everyone says that romance is dying. I'm romantic." While the responses of the other characters to her morbid proclamations range from interest to concern to tolerance, Carroll recognizes the deception but accepts it as an aspect of her personality. It is worth noting that Cavell, in his essay "Psychoanalysis and Cinema: The Melodrama of the Unknown Woman," acknowledges Garbo as "the greatest, or the most fascinating, cinematic image on film of the unknown woman" (Cavell, 36). Allowing for the (perhaps intentional) redundancy, Garbo remains a symbol of alienation and one that Karen attempts to live up to throughout the film, although in Garbo's case her "unknowingness" becomes equated with independence, whereas in Karen's case it is indicative of insecurity.

While Karen seeks to maintain the role of unknown woman in her relationships with both Ken and Carroll, Rudolph's other female characters seem equally "unknown," both to themselves and to those around them, especially the male characters. When photographer Nona first goes to see agent Susan Moore early in the film, she knocks on the office door and Susan asks, "Who's there?" to which Nona responds, "I haven't figured that out yet." Like the others, Nona is involved in a search, and her inquiry manifests itself in taking pictures of corners (and, as Carl proudly points out, she makes sense of them too). We get the feeling that she finds these empty corners more revealing than empty relationships, particularly the one she is having with Carl. When Carroll asks if she really cares about his father, her only response is "He cares about me."

Susan, like Nona, is successful professionally but seems to have been unable to enter into a fulfilling personal relationship. She, too, appears to have been involved with both Carl and Carroll. She has lost Carl to

Nona and also loses Carroll, however briefly, to Nona as well. Ann is another professionally successful woman who masks the insecurity of her failing marriage by claiming to be independent. As she drives Carroll to the house she has rented for him, she tells him she likes Los Angeles because "you get to choose who you want to be and how you want to live." The concept of "unknowingness" and deception is established in an early party scene when Susan meets Ann and tells her she pictured her differently based on her voice on the phone. Although she is married to Jack, Ann becomes attracted to Carroll. She even becomes jealous of what she perceives as the sexually overt come-on of Carroll's live-in housekeeper, Linda. Ironically, while Linda has a sexual encounter with Jack (and has no objection to taking money for it), Carroll is one of the few men with whom she does not become involved. Linda appears to be the most independent and uninhibited of the female characters, but she reveals her insecurity during an early conversation with Ken (another of her potential clients) when he tells her, "Those are choices you have to make," and she responds, "I like when you make my choices." Even her willingness to exploit the needs of the men she encounters by taking money has its price, as demonstrated when Jack assaults her and then demands his money's worth after paying her.

Ann Goode (Sally Kellerman) seeks temporary escape from her empty marriage in an equally unfulfilling affair with composer Carroll Barber (Keith Carradine) in "the city of one-night stands."
Courtesy Museum of Modern Art/Film Stills Archive.

While the film's female characters seek to define themselves through their relationships, Rudolph's male characters tend to use sexual interactions to mask their own insecurities and deficiencies. All of the male characters are depicted as financially and vocationally successful, with the exception of the seemingly aimless Carroll, a songwriter who has been brought back to Los Angeles on the pretext of writing songs for a new album that is actually an attempt at reconciliation by Carl. However, as indicated by the marriages of Jack and Ken, they have been less successful in their personal lives. Even Carroll's seeming "stud" role (clearly derived from his *Nashville* persona) is indicated as demonstrating an inability to make a commitment (at one point Nona even asks if he is ready to make a commitment, and he responds, "Maybe").

It is Carroll's character that has raised the greatest objections from feminist critics, who view Rudolph's use of the character as a chauvinistic device to solve the problems of the women in the film. Such an interpretation, however, drastically oversimplifies the responses of the women to their relationship with Carroll and their subsequent understanding of their own needs as a result. This interpretation also fails to take into account Carroll's own transformation as a result of these interactions and his awareness of the emptiness of his life. Carroll's stud posturing becomes another form of the deception Karen warns about at the start of the film. The women he encounters do not resolve their problems because they sleep with him, but rather they discover that such brief liaisons are unsatisfactory and do not provide them with the fulfillment they seek. Carroll comes to the same realization at the end of the film, as he listens to Karen talking to Ken on the phone.

Although it does not end up at the same point as the films discussed in Cavell's study of remarriage comedies, the relationship of Karen and Ken uses a number of elements identified as characteristic of the genre. The most direct allusion to the remarriage comedies identified by Cavell comes in the use of a photo album Karen sends to Ken, which depicts their earlier, happier relationship. The album is clearly an attempt to recapture that relationship, and the two discuss this on the phone near the end of the film. The photo album functions in much the same way as the home movies in George Cukor's *Adam's Rib* of 1949 (another film about people whose professional success interferes with their personal lives), and this earlier film is directly recalled in one of the photos of Ken clowning for the camera, which matches a shot of Spencer Tracy in the same pose in one of the home movies. Whereas the characters in the films identified by Cavell work through their reconciliation in a "green world" away from their normal environment, it is a significant demonstration of Rudolph's variation on the genre that the reconciliation between Karen and Ken is incomplete, with Karen's suggestion that they move to a place in the country (a notion again inspired by the Garbo film) seemingly meeting with some resistence from Ken. It is also worth noting that their attempt at analyzing their relationship occurs not through direct confrontation, as in earlier examples of the remarriage genre, but over the phone (a key motif in many Rudolph films and one that is most prominently employed in *Choose Me*). The ultimate incompatibility of their relationship seems to be not a result of the male-female dichotomies of other screen couples but of a conflict of genres, with Ken identified with the hero of a remarriage comedy (most specifically Spencer Tracy) and Karen equated (as she does herself in her constant *Camille* references) with the heroine of a melodrama of the unknown woman.

In addition to the relationship of Karen and Ken, the other literal marriage in the film—between Ann and Jack—undergoes a pattern of separation and reunification. Their reconciliation, however, seems less the result of a process of remarriage and a new awareness of their relationship than of a feeling that each has no place left to go. The reconciliation takes the form of a physical encounter, with no attempt made to discuss the more cerebral aspects of their relationships, and indicates that they will probably continue to pursue extramarital affairs while maintaining the facade of marriage.

Another major relationship in the film that seeks some form of resolution is between Carroll and his father, Carl. While the traditions of classical comedy from which Cavell derived his genre of remarriage placed an emphasis on the relationship between father and daughter, Rudolph sidesteps the Oedipal implications of parent-child relationships (except in the sense that father and son both become involved with the same woman) and employs the relationship between Carroll and Carl not to create complications for spousal relationships but to comment on attitudes toward success in society. Carl desires a son who will follow in his business interests, and while Ken acts as surrogate (a role he seems all too eager to fill), Carl acknowledges that this is not the same. The lack of commitment Carroll has demonstrated in his personal life seems to have extended to his professional work, and his appearance in L.A. is the result of machinations on the part of Susan and Carl (in an apparent attempt

at some kind of revenge for his dismissal of her, Susan later informs
Carroll that his songs were forced on Eric and that he has been
bought and merchandised).

In this case the conflict in the relationship between father and son
does not result in any acknowledged reconciliation but does lead to
change on Carroll's part. Rather than embracing his father's notions
of success, he demonstrates his own artistic integrity when, after Eric
has decided not to do the album, Carroll goes into the studio and
records his songs himself. As the credits roll, the camera does a slow
arc around Carroll, ending on a medium close-up profile shot and
tightening to a close-up as Carroll turns to the camera. Although the
image freezes at this point, the final movement equates him with
Karen through his direct acknowledgment of the camera, suggesting
that he is now the one who will begin to undergo the process of self-
reflection. Carroll has already indicated his shattering of his old identity when, as he leaves his rented home to go to the studio, he gives
Linda his hat, his liquor flask, and his house keys. As the director
acknowledged when discussing Carradine's character, "He's naive,
but he's avoiding what he's after throughout most of the film. He just
doesn't want to deal with anything. At the end of the film he just
makes a simple, little statement and a little choice, simple in terms of
what's going on and the way we see it" (Macklin, 10). More significantly, Carroll's final assertion of artistic independence anticipates a
number of artists in later Rudolph films who find themselves caught
between deception and artistic expression.

In presenting his admittedly complex structure, Rudolph uses a
visual style that isolates combinations or groupings of characters to
demonstrate their changing relationships. Although dealing with several characters, Rudolph seldom opts for the kinds of expansive
shots, characteristic of Altman, in which several people are shown
interacting at once. As he had done in his two earlier directorial
efforts, Rudolph uses a number of two-shots and then alienates the
characters still further by panning or zooming to focus on one of
them. Even in group scenes, such as an early party scene at Jack's
house or the later "coming out" party for Carroll, Rudolph tends to
draw attention to relationships between two individuals. In the latter
scene, for example, Carl and Carroll go outside to detach themselves
from the crowd as they argue. Their discussion is followed by a cut to
a close-up of Nona, who has been involved with both of them.

Rudolph also employs mise-en-scène to emphasize the triangular
relationships. During a session at the recording studio that serves as a

nucleus at which the lives of several of the characters intertwine, Carroll and Nona are seen kissing on the left side of the screen, while Susan observes them on the right. The design of the studio emphasizes their physical separation and reinforces the emotional distance between Carroll and Susan (the recording studio will be used in a number of later films to emphasize separation, often in contrast to the intimacy and unity of characters during shots of live performances). The shot is echoed a short time later when Carroll and Nona embrace in a taxi while Karen watches from the curb.

In interviews Rudolph has indicated that his inspiration for the visual design of the film was the painter Jack Beal. An aspect of Beal's work that may have influenced Rudolph is his use of mirrors as visual metaphor (Beal's 1966 painting *Sondra in Three Vanity Mirrors* is echoed in a shot of Susan viewing her multiple reflection). Mirrors figure prominently in 17 scenes, and the actual number of shots in which they appear is significantly higher. While the extensive use of such shots might be regarded as the indulgence of a novice director, the motif serves as a literal reflection of the characters' search for identity. Whereas mirrors have been used by directors such as Jean Cocteau, Joseph Losey, and Orson Welles in a baroque manner to distort or to create a different reality, Rudolph uses them as a function of his characters' psychoanalytical search for self-understanding. This concept of self-reflection is extended through Karen's direct address to the camera, which calls attention to the self-reflexive nature of cinema.

Individuals are seen looking into or reflected in mirrors at points in which they are trying to understand themselves and their own actions. The examination by characters of their reflections is most apparent during their phone calls to potential sexual partners, as though they are attempting to define themselves through these relationships. After their initial meeting, Karen and Carroll are both seen reflected in mirrors while they converse on the phone, and Karen tries to make Carroll understand that she is not what he needs. Significantly, following the return of many of these characters to their original pairings and a suggestion of the potential for reconciliation, there are no mirror shots, as though this return to the original "marriage" (to use Cavell's term) has led to an understanding of self that no longer requires, or perhaps allows for, reflection.

In addition to reinforcing the concept of self-reflection, mirrors are used to fragment, indicating that characters are not completely whole. As Ann drives Carroll to his rented home, only her eyes are initially seen reflected in the rear-view mirror. The early shot of Susan talking on the phone while reflected in multiple mirrors not only serves to fragment her but also suggests that there are several facets to her personality that need to be examined.

Another aspect of the structure of the film—and one that functions in both visual and aural terms—is the use of repetition. Carroll's sexual exploits are often telegraphed by two-shots of him and one of the female leads sharing his ever-present bottle of liquor. An even more direct use of repetition occurs in the dialogue, suggesting that the characters have learned to communicate through rote recitation rather than through genuine interaction with the person to whom they are speaking. Even the film's title becomes an empty salutation mechanically repeated by various characters. Karen repeats the same phrases to a number of different characters, including the aforementioned Goya quote ("The sleep of reason produces monsters"). Her husband, Ken, first tells Linda that the two of them can go far beyond a normal man-woman relationship (raising the question of what is considered a "normal" man-woman relationship and how it is possible for a couple to go beyond it) and later tells the same thing to Karen when they are attempting a reconciliation. At one point, when a phone rings Karen's voice is heard off-screen saying not to answer it because it is probably a wrong number—or the great romance of her life. When Carroll tries to call Karen at home after she has rejected him, Ken tells her not to answer it, and she again comments that it is probably a wrong number (although, significantly, she leaves off the addendum to her earlier observation). Karen answers the phone and tries to pretend it is a wrong number, but Ken calls her a phony after she hangs up. Later, when Karen and Carroll finally get together, Ken calls Carroll's number and Carroll tells her not to answer. She does, however, and hands the phone to Carroll, suggesting that she wants Ken to know she is with Carroll and is using him to force her husband toward reconciliation. The scene is repeated a short time later when Karen (who in earlier scenes has been depicted carrying on a telephone conversation even after the other party has hung up or starting one before picking up the phone) continues to mumble about the connection between the words *phone* and *phony* in an isolated shot, while Carroll is heard talking into the phone off-screen.

The use of repeated dialogue when employed by the same person indicates how much each person remains the same, despite attempts at internal reflection and efforts to change; but it is also used to establish connections between characters who repeat the same phrases. The connection between characters is reinforced more obviously in the similarity of names (Goode, Hood, Wood or Karen, Carroll, Carl, Ken), which suggest that several of these characters are parts of a larger entity and need one another to become whole. The concept is even reinforced, though doubtless less intentionally, in the repeated consonance of the names of the actors who play these parts (Carradine, Considine, Kellerman, Keitel).

Repetition in dialogue on the part of an individual character indicates an inability to escape from established patterns. Ken provides evidence that he is attempting to understand the unknown woman to whom he is married by suggesting that he and Karen go to a Garbo film together, yet during his attempt at reconciliation he repeats the line he said earlier to Linda. Following the conversation between Karen and Ken (which Linda cuts short by disconnecting the phone after hearing the familiar line about going beyond a normal man-woman relationship), Karen has a conversation with Linda in which she repeats her comments about not having long to live and once again quotes Goya. Despite her contention that people change, she falls back into the familiar pattern. Her opening observations about deception are even reinforced when she tells Linda her name is Marguerite, the heroine of the Garbo film she admires (to which Linda responds that she has also been using a different name, reinforcing Karen's initial contention that people deceive themselves).

In its complexity of construction and multiplicity of characters, *Welcome to L.A.* seems an especially audacious project for what was, for all intents and purposes, a debut film. Particularly impressive is the dexterity with which Rudolph is able to define characters and their relationships in the film's early stages (an ability that was no doubt greatly enhanced by his work on *Nashville*). Critics who objected to the film tended to do so on the grounds that the characters lacked emotional depth and that the director made little use of the title location, restricting his focus to his main characters and providing no sense of a larger social context. It is the city itself, however, that seems to have been responsible for draining the characters of their emotions. Rudolph emphasizes their alienation by placing them in a landscape devoid of life. He has indicated that this approach was deliberate, because he wanted to avoid exteriors and deal with the interiors of his characters (much like Woody Allen's appropriately titled *Interiors* of the next year [1978]). He also makes little use of the Christmastime setting, and this lack of attention only serves to emphasis the detachment of the characters and their desperation. Christmas becomes a symbol not of redemption but of commercialization and the spiritual emptiness of the characters. Rudolph is already establishing the concept that people have learned to replace real emotions with synthetic ones, and it is only by getting in touch with themselves and their true feelings that they have any hope of redemption.

In Rudolph's summation of the film he claims that

> it's like emotional science fiction. It's dealing with people who can't seem to deal with their own problems. And yet all these people, they're doing it out of their own best interests. They really want to satisfy that need. They want to be loved. They really want to be loved and they want to love. The women all get stripped down, figuratively and then once literally, and the men just keep doing the opposite. So that how can these two people ever communicate? This race, men and women, where's that line of communication? It's about merchandising of people and how when you get to a certain level you can be bought. . . . What we've done in the film hopefully is we've examined these people who have the opportunity to face themselves first. You can't face anybody else until you do that first. We create all these situations so that [these characters are] really pushed into places that they shouldn't be, and they have to bust out by facing themselves. Some people miss that altogether. (Macklin, 9)

CHAPTER 3

Remember My Name:
There Is Buddha and There Is Pest

If a woman possesses manly virtues one should run away from her; and if
she does not possess them she runs away from herself.
    —Friedrich Nietzsche, "Maxims and Arrows" (*Twilight of the Idols,* 1889)

After *Welcome to L.A.* Rudolph turned his attention to the script for
The Moderns, which he hoped to make in Paris (although the film
was not produced until 1988). He was contacted by Altman, who was
looking for projects to produce under the auspices of his company
Lion's Gate. Rudolph claims he developed the idea for *Remember My
Name* (1978) while driving to meet with Altman, after passing a theater marquee announcing "femme fatale" films with Joan Crawford
and Rita Hayworth.

These origins define the generic territory of the film, although
once again Rudolph has placed the formula within the context of a
contemporary triangular relationship. In keeping with the noir
atmosphere, Rudolph adopts a visual style that appears to be modeled after the canvases of painter Edward Hopper, and the Hopperesque nightscapes provide a perfect background of the depiction
of its working-class characters, ably supported by the blues soundtrack of Alberta Hunter. While not motivated by one character in the
way Baskin's songs were identified as the product of Keith Carradine's character in *Welcome to L.A.,* Hunter's songs become associated with Emily and serve to externalize her emotional states.

23

The reference to past films is appropriate to a story of people trying to come to terms with past lives. If Baskin's lyrics in *Welcome to L.A.* suggest that Rudolph's characters are bearing the burden of previous relationships that are largely unidentified, a past relationship becomes the motivating force for the main character in *Remember My Name*. As played by Geraldine Chaplin, Emily expands on the character of Karen in Rudolph's previous film. Whereas Karen seems uncertain about whether to define herself in terms of her relationships with others (particularly her marriage to Ken) or through the establishment of her own personal identity, Emily manages to come to terms with a past marital relationship as a part of the process of redefining herself.

The story presents a traditional triangular structure, with the remarried Neil (Anthony Perkins) confronted by the release of his first wife, Emily, from prison. As in other Rudolph works, this central situation is complicated by additional relationships, although the levels of complexity are not as extreme as in *Welcome to L.A.* While functioning in more than one triangular configuration, Emily's goal, which is only gradually revealed as the film progresses, is not the attainment of a satisfactory relationship for herself but the alienation of Neil from both of the women in his life.

The characters in *Welcome to L.A.* are entrapped by their own inability to make commitments or to see beyond themselves. *Remember My Name* provides a more literal depiction of entrapment, and it is this first literal and then figurative confinement from which Emily must escape. Although her experience in prison is never shown on screen, it becomes a key element and is implied at the start of the film, through the prison sound effects that are heard before the opening credits or even the studio logo appears on screen.

While Chaplin's Emily may be no more sure of her identity than Karen as the film begins, she is depicted as more in control of her environment. Chaplin is once again first seen in a car, but this time she is the one behind the wheel. Yet Emily's confused identity is also implied in the opening by the fragmented image presented of her, with only her hands initially visible as she drives. When Emily stops the car and gets out, the camera remains inside, shooting through the windshield as she walks in front of the car, and her face is visible for the first time in profile while she smokes a cigarette (an object that will take on symbolic connotations throughout the film and is most often associated with Emily's attitude of defiance). As Emily returns to the car to follow Neil (unknown to him), she is again fragmented, with only her eyes visible in the mirror on the side of the car.

Much of the early part of the film is concerned with Emily's attempts to redefine her image, which she hopes will lead to her escape from the entrapment of her past, of which Neil is gradually revealed to be a part. Before beginning her transformation, Emily examines the environments in which Neil and his second wife, Barbara (Berry Berenson), operate. Neil is in the construction business, and both the skeletal constructions of the houses on which he is working and the home with which his wife is associated provide their own representations of the theme of entrapment. Indeed, Neil's job represents a world in which not only the characters but the environment itself seems to be continually reconstructing itself. Emily's attempt at a reconstruction of her own life is telegraphed as she walks past a store bearing a sign stating "Coming Soon—Brand New Image."

In *Remember My Name* (1978), Neil (Anthony Perkins) comforts Emily (Geraldine Chaplin) after visiting her in jail. Despite their embrace, Neil remains aloof, and the composition suggests the emotional distance between them.
Courtesy Film Center of Chicago.

Emily's first step in her reimaging is the purchase of a new wardrobe. In the dress shop Rudolph indicates that the entrapment felt by his lead character can be extended metaphorically to the treatment of all women in society, as the mannequins in the shop are shown wearing handcuffs and black blindfolds, an image of oppression that women are apparently effectively marketing and selling to themselves. The camera stays on Emily as she examines herself in a mirror in the shop while trying on her new purchases. Having made her decisions, she arranges for the packages to be wrapped. She will later open them in her room as though they were gifts from a friend, in essence a present from the person who was her former self.

The rooming house where Emily is staying provides the first indication that more than a new wardrobe and a new attitude will be required for Emily's transformation to be complete. The building is first seen through bars, which reinforce the concept of imprisonment. Rudolph again employs mirrors for their symbolic potential, as Emily discovers the mirror in her room has been shattered and provides a distorted, incomplete image. At night, her sleep is troubled by recurring visual and aural reminders of prison.

Emily begins to perform small acts of vengeance to shatter the seemingly serene existence of Neil and Barbara. As in the relationship of Karen and Ken in *Welcome to L.A.,* however, Rudolph suggests that there is a certain amount of tension between the married couple even before Emily's presence is known (the connection of Neil to Ken is even made briefly in a bedroom scene in which Neil is wearing the same kind of yellow shorts worn by Ken in the earlier film). The tension is marginally addressed in a shot of Barbara answering a phone call from Neil on one side of a wall, while her parents are visible on the other side playing cards. After the call, Barbara leans against the wall, and her mother questions if there is something wrong between her and Neil.

Emily begins lurking outside Neil's house, watching him and his wife. In an early indication of her violent tendencies, she tears up the flowers outside their front door, leaving them in Barbara's car. Any sense that this might be a random act is shattered, literally, when Emily (in an action that echoes the shattered mirror in her room) throws a rock through a window of their house at night while Neil and Barbara are making love. When Neil rushes out to investigate, Emily runs away, but pauses long enough to make sure he gets a look at her before driving off.

Emily returns to her room to discover that the super, Pike (Moses Gunn), has brought her a new lamp and a mirror to replace the fragmented one. While these objects might suggest both illumination and a complete reflection of her new image, it is Pike who reminds her, when Emily comments that she wants to make her new house livable, that "you have to make it livable yourself." An uneasy relationship develops between the former convict and the super, who represents authority, as demonstrated when Emily crawls on the floor and begs him for clean sheets and drapes, reverting back to her imprisoned state in a state prison. When Pike tries to pick her up from the floor, Emily yells, "Don't you dare kiss me," then covers her mouth and first slaps and the hugs Pike. It is Pike who addresses the "unknowingness" of women when he comments, "Takes a woman to take a man out of himself. But to do it, she's got to be better than him."

Emily's early acts of vengeance, which seem aimed as much at Barbara as at Neil, suggest a traditional femme fatale development. This is most evident in an extended scene in which Emily prowls around Neil and Barbara's home while Barbara is in the house but unaware of her presence. Emily eventually corners Barbara in the kitchen and begins repeating everything Barbara says. This not only represents another instance of Rudolph's use of repetition as an aspect of language but also foreshadows the eventual role reversal of the two women. The lack of any physical attack (although both women are holding knives) demonstrates that Emily's form of revenge will be much more complex than that enacted by her cinematic sisters, such as Gene Tierney in *Leave Her to Heaven* (1945).

Emily's most violent actions are not directed at Neil or Barbara but at Rita (Alfre Woodard), a co-worker at the department store where Emily gets a job as a clerk and who is spreading stories about Emily having served time in prison. When Rita's boyfriend tries to stop Emily from getting into her car, she stabs him in the armpit with a pencil. The attack is witnessed by Barbara, and she reports it to Emily's boss. Emily also smashes into Neil's stalled truck and allows him to get another good look at her before driving away. After she returns home, Emily is arrested not for the stabbing, which is what she assumes, but for the earlier window-breaking incident. She is taken away in the rooming house's cagelike elevator, once again reinforcing the entrapment motif.

When Neil and Barbara arrive at the jail house, he asks to see Emily alone and the details of their past association are revealed. Hints of the remarriage formula surface, as Emily refers to Neil by a nickname and makes other references that apparently only the two of them share. It is revealed that Emily was imprisoned for killing Neil's mistress (Neil later tells Barbara it was an accident that only looked like murder) and that Neil has not informed Barbara about his previous marriage. During their encounter in jail, Emily seeks comfort from Neil, but he hesitates and remains aloof when she embraces him. The camera remains on his face, with Emily below the bottom of the frame as she tells him that thoughts of him kept her alive while she was in prison. "I'm the most important thing in your life," Emily says, as though reassuring herself of her own importance, and then alludes to her own past dependence when she adds, "Remember, you told me that." Following their meeting, Neil elects not to press charges and suggests the connection between the two women and their unknown qualities when he refers to "my wife . . . my other wife." Neil later tries to explain his past association with Emily to Barbara, but in keeping with the darker tone of the film the discussion leads not to reconciliation but to separation. Throughout the remainder of the film Barbara will gradually take on habits of Emily, suggesting that she, too, is attempting to re-create herself and to find some sense of identity beyond that which her marriage provided.

Emily comes to visit Neil at the construction site, and as they talk she sits in one of the partially constructed houses, the beams and studs of the unfinished structure indicating that a renewal of their relationship will become another form of entrapment for both of them. Nevertheless, the two retreat to the "green world" of a Hopperesque bar, where they reminisce about the past while working their way through the drink list. Eventually, they end up in bed together at Emily's room. As Alberta Hunter sings "The Love I Have for You" on the soundtrack, a close-up of Emily's face during their lovemaking is followed by a cut to a shot of Barbara framed in the window of her house.

In a development that recalls Ingmar Bergman's *Persona* (1966), the two women begin to exchange identities, and the transformation becomes complete in the film's final scenes. Emily leaves Neil asleep in her room (the camera filming through chicken wire as she exits the building to indicate that her escape is not yet complete and that his entrapment has just begun) and returns to the dress shop, where she purchases nearly $700 worth of clothes under Barbara's name and seems to take satisfaction in the clerk referring to her as Neil's wife. As she prepares to leave, the clerk asks if she also wants to take the nondescript gray dress she has been wearing since her release from prison, and Emily tells her it never fit right anyway. Barbara, by contrast, is seen smoking a cigarette and drinking beer as she watches television, adopting the tough attitude of defiance earlier expressed by Emily. She has also taken to wearing dark glasses, an image that will become associated in later Rudolph films with the disintegration of a relationship (Stella in *Love at Large* puts them on after watching Harry kiss Miss Dolan, and Joyce wears them in *Mortal Thoughts* after her husband's murder).

Emily stops briefly to say good-bye to Pike and give him her keys, during which Rudolph provides a shot of her hand, indicating that (despite her earlier identification of herself in the dress shop as Neil's wife) she has removed her wedding band. She is last seen changing into new clothes at the side of the road and then driving away. The ending credits roll over a shot of the apartment building through bars as the camera slowly zooms in to the window of the prison from which she has now escaped, and in which she has left Neil. While a direct transformation takes place between the two women, with Emily literally taking Barbara's name and Barbara adopting her mannerisms, Emily also undergoes a kind of spiritual transposition with Neil, freeing herself but leaving him in a symbolic prison.

Emily (Geraldine Chaplin) prepares to leave after spending the night with Neil (Anthony Perkins), enacting a psychological rather than a violent form of revenge. The bars behind them suggest a prison from which she will escape and in which he has been trapped.
Courtesy Museum of Modern Art/Film Stills Archive.

The plot line and events of *Remember My Name* are more stream-lined than those of *Welcome to L.A.,* and the director has acknowl-edged that it is a more focused work. But the film incorporates a number of elements from the earlier film. Rudolph again employs his characteristic device of beginning on a two-shot and moving to a tighter shot that isolates one of the characters. Barbara's first aware-ness of an outside threat occurs when she and a neighbor return to her house just after Emily has uprooted her flowers. From a two-shot of Barbara and the neighbor, Rudolph moves to an isolated shot of Barbara as she discovers the damage. The action is repeated a short time later, when Barbara is talking to Neil, and Rudolph moves from a two-shot to a close-up of her as she tells him, "I love you." Both of these shots emphasize Barbara's growing sense of isolation, which will eventually result in her adopting the personality traits of Emily in order to survive. At other points, Rudolph indicates Barbara's sense of isolation through the composition of a shot, as when the walls of Barbara's house separate her from her parents and later from Emily after the other woman sneaks inside.

Rudolph also employs repetition as an aspect of both character and structure. Early in the film Emily rehearses the speech she will make to Neil and then begins to recite it verbatim when the two finally meet. She taunts Barbara when she confronts her in the house by repeating everything Barbara says, which also sets up the eventual per-sonality transference of the two women. Parallel elements within the structure of the film include the use of black female characters associated with the white female leads: the black neighbor provides a source of support for Barbara, whereas the black co-worker serves as a source of conflict for Emily.

In addition to techniques Rudolph employed in his previous film, *Remember My Name* shows the emergence of new aspects of his work. Visually he uses more direct dream imagery, particularly in Emily's recollections of her prison experience, which emerge as vague, defocused shadows and distorted sounds while she is sleeping in her new environment. Although Emily remains the major focus of the story and instigates most of the events depicted, Rudolph pro-vides a few instances that call into question traditional notions of viewpoint. When Barbara is first seen returning home, her arrival is shot from inside the house: the camera pans to follow her car as she drives up, pauses as she gets out, and then pans to the door as she enters the house, creating the feeling that she is being watched. This would seem to imply that Emily is inside waiting for her, but the phone is ringing as Barbara enters the house, and the caller turns out to be Emily, whom we discover in the next shot is calling from a nearby phone booth. The defining of each character's space leaves unanswered the question of whose viewpoint motivated the shots of Barbara's return home. The apparent ability of characters to exist in two places at the same time is a situation that Rudolph will incorporate more directly and audaciously in later films, particularly so in *Choose Me.*

Perhaps in response to criticisms of *Welcome to L.A.,* Rudolph offers suggestions of a larger social context for the events depicted. Although focus is again restricted to a select group of characters, Emily's attempts to reenter society indicate the presence of a power structure. This is most evident in her interactions with her boss (Jeff Goldblum), who is seeking to come to terms with his own past. Rudolph contrasts the intimate personal drama being played out by the main characters with a large-scale tragedy, indicated only by the continual television reports concerning an earthquake in Budapest. These reports not only provide for some humorous wordplay ("There is Buddha and there is pest," one commentator solemnly proclaims), but they act as a constant reminder of a larger world outside of the self-contained universe in which the principal characters operate, where tragedies of almost unfathomable proportions occur. The earthquake references also indicate destruction, in contrast to the concepts of construction and reconstruction associated with the lead characters.

Although not as overt as the political proclamations of Hal Philip Walker in *Nashville,* the broadcast chatter in the background provides often inane reflections on the events in the film. At one point Neil watches television (shortly after Barbara has been confronted in the kitchen by Emily) while an announcer drones on about the need for a man to escape within himself and forget the problems of the past. At the end of the film, following her transformation into the cigarette-smoking, beer-guzzling unknown woman, Barbara watches television as the death toll in the earthquake is reported to be more than one million, and the announcer incongruously comments on the need for us to realize our potential as human beings.

The most significant element that *Remember My Name* adds to the Rudolph worldview is the establishment of a climate in which violence is possible at any time. While violence in *Welcome to L.A.* is limited to a few angry verbal exchanges and Jack's spontaneous assault of Linda, *Remember My Name* creates an atmosphere where love and violence are inseparable (as demonstrated most directly in Emily's relationship with Pike). This atmosphere will inform many of Rudolph's later works and cause the romantic comedy and film noir aspects of these two early films to merge.

Although Rudolph has suggested that the film is "a metaphor for whatever impact the women's movement as a public forum had on me," he also acknowledged the criticism it drew from female viewers: "They said Emily . . . was too much like a man in her vengeance. I pointed out that if she were like a man, she would have killed her ex-husband, and shame on them for not understanding that" (Rudolph 1985, 264). In retrospect, Emily's revenge is more psychological than physical and is a good deal less violent than that of many of the hero-ines of the noir films that inspired Rudolph's work, or of the female leads in the director's later *Mortal Thoughts.* It might also be argued that it is Emily's masculine traits that she must resolve before her transformation to a new identity can be complete. By contrast, by the end of the film Barbara has broken out of the imprisonment of a tra-ditional woman's role by adopting characteristics associated not only with Emily at the outset of the film but also with men.

In comparing Rudolph's first two major efforts as a director, critic Tom Milne regarded *Remember My Name* as a much more assured work than *Welcome to L.A.* (a view the director shares). In an article in *Sight and Sound,* Milne stated, "*Remember My Name* is a brilliantly realized exercise in classical disciplines. In place of the elaborately intellectualized schema of *Welcome to L.A.,* a unilaterally straight-forward revenge plot that might have served as a Joan Crawford vehi-cle; instead of the portentous sociological comment offered by Richard Baskin's songs, the eloquent simplicity of Alberta Hunter's blues. Again an unreal world—separate burrows, or urban solitude and domestic bliss, connected with serpentine menace by the trajec-tory of Geraldine Chaplin's car coming from one to destroy the other—whose emotional truth becomes devastatingly real."[1] When Rudolph again returned to independent filmmaking with *Choose Me,* he created another "unreal world," but in this unreal world his female characters share traits of the women in *Welcome to L.A.* and *Remember My Name* by seeking both satisfactory relationships and personal independence.

CHAPTER 4

Choose Me:
Trying to Get Back the Blood

For the night
Shows stars and women in a better light.
—Lord Byron, *Don Juan* (1819-25)

Choose Me (1984) marked Rudolph's return to a more personal style of filmmaking after a period of working on two studio projects and *Return Engagement,* a 1983 documentary about G. Gordon Liddy and Timothy Leary. Considered by many critics to be one of the best films of the 1980s, *Choose Me* was the director's most successful film to date and the one in which film writers began to become more aware of Rudolph's worldview. *Choose Me* actually provides a synthesis of concepts established in *Welcome to L.A.* and *Remember My Name,* incorporating the romantic rondelay and deceptions of the first film with the potential for violence and indications of the effects of the past on present relationships in the second. The film also demonstrates the move toward the creation of a self-contained and undefined universe, whose identity only becomes apparent at night (although shot in Los Angeles, the location is not identified by name as it had been in the title of Rudolph's earlier film). The incorporation of aspects of both films is most evident in the progression of two of the female characters, Eve (Lesley Ann Warren) and Dr. Nancy Love (Genevieve Bujold), with one finding at least potential satisfaction in a marital relationship, while the other gains independence and a new sense of identity outside of relationships with men. Both women become involved with yet another of Keith Carradine's stud characters, but in keeping with the film's overall tone, even this role is examined for its potential humor. Unlike the underlying narcissism of Carroll in *Welcome to L.A.*, Carradine's presentation has a certain innocence, despite his allegedly convoluted past.

Rudolph has described the film as a triangle with five corners—a situation further complicated by many of these "corners" adopting dual identities. Radio sex therapist Dr. Nancy Love, a kind of Gallic Dr. Ruth, becomes roommates with Eve, but to protect her professonal identity she gives her name as Ann. Eve, the owner of a bar that bears her name, has been seeking advice from Dr. Love, using a variety of aliases in her telephone conversation. She is involved in an affair with Zack (Patrick Bauchau), who is married to the poetic Pearl (Rae Dawn Chong). Pearl frequents Eve's without letting on that she is aware of the affair, hoping to catch her husband and Eve together, and she also occasionally calls Dr. Love using an alias. Into this already convoluted construction comes Mickey (Keith Carradine), recently released from a mental institution. While the women all adopt roles for one another, Mickey either represents the one honest character or the most extreme case of deception among the protagonists. He is identified at the hospital as a pathological liar, but he insists that he always tells the truth. Rudolph does not allow even the viewer to penetrate this deception. At one point Nancy/Ann attempts to determine the truth by going through his belongings, but the materials she finds do not clarify whether he is telling the truth or has gone to elaborate lengths to establish a false identity.

In addition to structural similarities to *Welcome to L.A.* and actor Keith Carradine as the lead who becomes involved with each of the female characters, Rudolph provides some direct allusions to the earlier film in the dialogue. Both during and after her sexual encounter with Mickey, Nancy/Ann refers to confusing feelings brought on by the wine with feelings in the blood. Later she tells one of her callers about "that uncontrollable impulse that shakes you to your very foundation, that makes your nerve ends tickle and your head spin and makes you feel like . . . like jelly. You may think it's wine, Rita, but it's not . . . it's blood, and there's nothing wrong with that feeling." The comments are a clear recapitulation of a line in one of Baskin's songs for *Welcome to L.A.* in which he equates drinking wine with "tryin' to get back the blood."

Along with its parallels to his earlier work, *Choose Me* shows similarities to the films selected by Cavell as representative of the comedy of remarriage. The use of the name Eve for the central female character recalls the heroine of Preston Sturges's *The Lady Eve* (1941), another woman who adopts disguises and enters into relationships for personal gain rather than mutual satisfaction (one might also draw a connection to the deceiving title character of *All about Eve* (1950), a movie whose poster is part of the décor in Pearl and Zack's apartment). Like Sturges, Rudolph toys with the idea of presenting a variation on the Garden of Eden story (as in the references to Adams and Garden streets), and on one level the film deals with Eve's redemption through her relationship with Mickey. The use of a threatened suicide as a means of bluffing out one's partner during the climactic standoff between Mickey and Eve recalls Spencer Tracy's bluff with a licorice gun in *Adam's Rib*. Even the final shot of Mickey and Eve on the bus to Las Vegas provides an obvious parallel to *It Happened One Night*.

In his complex geometric pattern Rudolph offers several potential candidates for both the remarriage and unknown woman formulas. Along with the obvious marital disparity between Pearl and Zack that needs to be resolved, there are references to Mickey's two previous marriages and to Eve's inability to sustain a relationship. The responses of Eve and Nancy/Ann to their encounter with Mickey become reflections of Cavell's two genres. Eve finds in this interaction a marital relationship that she believes she will be capable of sustaining. Nancy/Ann, on the other hand, becomes more aware of herself through her brief liaison with Mickey and becomes less concerned with developing a relationship than with employing her newfound sexual knowledge.

Nancy/Ann's role as an unknown woman even works variations on the concept of parents and children, which Cavell regards as an important characteristic of the genre. As Dr. Love, she acts as parent to her listeners and makes reference on more than one occasion to the tremendous responsibility their dependence on her represents. Nancy herself takes on the role of child, however, when talking on the phone to the psychiatrist who clearly functions as an authority figure for her, although he is never seen (the voice is by John Considine, providing another connection to *Welcome to L.A.*).

If Nancy/Ann shares attributes of the unknown woman, the relationship between Mickey and Eve follows the pattern of a remarriage comedy. Like the couple in *Bringing up Baby* (1938), one of the films discussed in Cavell's text, they have not been married to each other before, but there is a sense of a past life that needs to be recaptured in order for their relationship to be complete. Eve is acknowledged as a substitution for the original owner of the nightclub that bears her name (she claims she actually took over the club because she was walking down the street and saw a sign with her name on it). Mickey has come back to the club seeking the original Eve, with whom he had a relationship, and there is a feeling that the new Eve is on some level (if not a literal one) the same person.

Although the encounters both women have with Mickey lead to different outcomes, they become the means for helping each woman define what she wants. Eve tells Dr. Love over the phone at the beginning of the film that "my life's pretty good . . . stable . . . I know what I want," but this is clearly an indication of her self-deception, particularly because she is using a false name at the time. Despite her constant denial of marriage as a possibility (she claims she took over the bar because she felt that going into business had to be better than getting married, declaring, "I've ruined too many marriages to have one of my own"), her calls to Dr. Love indicate that she is not finding fulfillment in casual relationships. Nancy also practices self-deception through the advice she gives, which is not drawn from actual experience. Like Eve, her insistence that she is beginning to understand herself only demonstrates her lack of awareness of what she really wants. In contrast to these two women, Pearl knows that she is seeking to recapture the feelings she and Zack had that have been lost since they married, and she appears to be using Mickey to try to make Zack jealous in an effort to win him back. Yet she also practices deception by calling Dr. Love under an assumed name to discuss her problems.

As each of these characters seeks some understanding of her needs and desires, Rudolph employs characteristic camera devices to demonstrate their search for self-awareness. He again uses mirror shots, but with a variation that adds to the air of unreality and the self-reflexive nature of the work. Rudolph often opens on a reflected image and then provides a 180-degree pan to the actual image, resulting in an initial disorientation as to what is real and what is reflected. This technique appears most prominently in a shot of Mickey in the bathroom prior to his sexual encounter with Nancy/Ann, and later in the bedroom during this interaction. The technique not only acknowledges the self-reflection of the characters, but it also calls attention to the self-reflexive nature of cinema.

In *Choose Me* (1984), Dr. Nancy Love (Genevieve Bujold, left) attempts to explain her heightened emotional awareness to Eve (Lesley Ann Warren, right) after her encounter with Mickey. Rudolph makes characteristic use of a mirror as part of his mise-en-scène to reflect the characters' search for identity.
Courtesy Museum of Modern Art/Film Stills Archive.

Perhaps the most deliberately self-reflexive moment—and one that calls into question the ability to determine reality in the film—occurs in the shot I discussed in the Introduction, in which Eve talks on the phone to Dr. Love about her attraction to Mickey. While neither woman is aware that they are both talking about the same man, Rudolph establishes a bond between them, as Nancy/Ann becomes visible in the background momentarily while Eve is talking to her on the phone. This shot becomes a literal indication of an almost telepathic connection between the two women. Nancy/Ann's sudden appearance in Eve's apartment on the phrase "Yes, yes, the thrill, the thrill" also suggests an externalization of Nancy/Ann's newly acquired (or reacquired) awareness of her sexuality.

The concepts of introspection and externalization are reinforced through Rudolph's camera work. Nancy/Ann's internal search in particular becomes associated with inward tracking shots. The introduction to Nancy/Ann occurs through a tracking shot into the booth as she tells a caller, "There's really no mystery to sex, but there may be to her." (This line she will contradict after her encounter with Mickey, when she tells Pearl during a broadcast, "Sex is largely a mystery. There's no such thing as normal sex. Normal sex is largely a matter of statistics." The comment suggests that her new awareness of a side of herself previously unrevealed has also called into question the doctrines she has espoused in her professional practice.) When Nancy/Ann calls her psychiatrist from her car after making arrangements to move in with Eve, the camera again tracks in, as though attempting to penetrate what her psychological problems might be. In the scene in which Nancy talks to Pearl on the phone, the camera zooms in to her in the radio booth as she observes, "What may be normal for the vast majority is no criterion of behavior for the exceptional person." During the final scene of Nancy/Ann in the booth, the camera tracks out rather than in, and the movement coincides with her line to another caller, "I'm learning, Betty, like you and so many others. I'm devoting my life to learning about men and women."

Dr. Love (Genevieve Bujold) dispenses advice to a caller from the isolated anonymity of her radio booth.
Courtesy Museum of Modern Art/Film Stills Archive.

The most overt use of the moving camera in the film occurs in the scene in which Mickey comes to see Eve and discovers Nancy/Ann. After he cleans up in Eve's bathroom, Nancy/Ann invites him to join her for lunch, and during their conversation Rudolph continually pans and trucks, undercutting the dialogue and establishing at once a sense of interaction but also separation between the two characters, as well as a feeling of restlessness and anxiety. They begin by talking about Eve, with Mickey expressing his opinion that she is scared of herself and is a blink away from going off, while Nancy/Ann (who, as a therapist, should be in a position to judge people) insists that Eve is one of the more emotionally stable people she has met. The shot becomes tighter and the camera more restless as Mickey mentions Dr. Love and Nancy/Ann begins to discuss her in the third person, stating that she must live her life half-in and half-out of reality. The camera begins to pull back as Nancy/Ann concludes that Dr. Love must do eccentric things that have become quite normal to her. The restless camera not only reinforces her confusion about her own identity but also creates an atmosphere of sexual tension that culminates in Mickey pulling her chair closer to him and implying that their general discussion about sexual interaction is becoming more personal.[1]

Nancy/Ann's position as a radio sex therapist as well as a psychiatric patient plays both sides of the Freudian aspects that Cavell cites in his discussion of the unknown woman. The sense of "knowingness" is directly acknowledged in Nancy/Ann's second conversation with her psychiatrist. She states, "I'm beginning to understand myself better now, entering a more knowing phase. And I know that I remain my own worst enemy and I also know that I am my own savior. Because freedom means responsibility." She fondles her leg as she says this, establishing a connection between sex and her conceptions of both freedom and responsiblity. Ironically, when she finally explores that freedom with Mickey she seems incapable of taking any responsiblity. Her use of the third person in her conversation with him suggests that she is not responsible for what happens with him because it is actually occurring to another person. She later rejects his marriage proposal by claiming, "I've never loved anyone, and I don't think I can." Although Mickey offers, "I could teach you that, too. How to be crazy, how to be in love," Nancy/Ann rejects the proposition.

Nancy/Ann's denial of marriage suggests a parallel with Eve, who comments, "I don't think I can make marriage last with anyone." A bond has been established between the two women in the telephone conversation at the beginning of the film, when Eve (calling herself Jane) begins to ask Nancy about her life and the latter replies, "That's my life, Jane, and we're talking about yours." Nancy simplifies Eve's psychological problems by telling her, "With the dilemma you're in we could discuss sexual attitudes, early childhood—but the truth is that when you make changes you sometimes have to endure pain," and Eve responds, "You're my therapy."

The differences between the two women become apparent when they meet. While discussing the terms of their arrangement at Eve's lounge, Nancy/Ann observes, "I don't have much success with men," to which Eve replies, "I have too much." As in *Remember My Name,* the two women undergo a transference of identities, with Eve moving from a position of sexual awareness and independence to one of emotional commitment and co-dependence, while Nancy/Ann goes from this position of commitment/co-dependence (at least in terms of her radio listeners) to one of sexual awareness and independence. As Nancy/Ann becomes aware of her need to define herself outside of a relationship, Eve begins to believe in the possibility of marriage.

The transformation is apparent in the scene in which the two women confront each other about Mickey—a discussion that Nancy/Ann prefaces with the statement, "You don't know that much about me, Eve. . . . I'm a very complicated person." She then states, "From my point of view, I'm sure it's just sexual," adding, "This is new to me, this is a major breakthrough," and implying that sex is as good a way as any to know someone. Eve's anger over the other woman having slept with Mickey suggests she is no longer able to accept the concept of casual encounters without commitment, at least where Mickey is concerned. Although she claims, "I don't own him. I don't own any man, and I never have. And no man owns me," it is clear that by this point she would like to own and be owned by Mickey (who earlier told Nancy/Ann, "My wives own me"). It is worth noting that this statement is presented in an incomplete parallel structure that recalls a comment in *His Girl Friday* (1940), in which Hildy tells Walter, "You are no longer my husband an no longer my boss and you're not going to be my boss." Although she does not undergo a transformation of personalities with either of the other women, Pearl at least indicates a desire to do so, through her expressed wish to be Dr. Love and her attempts to catch Eve with Zack.

Mickey makes a connection with each of these women and also serves as a transitional figure between Eve and Nancy/Ann. Like

Nancy/Ann, he is "confused about his personality" and has undergone psychiatric evaluation. Interestingly, it is Nancy/Ann—who would seem in the best position to identify with his confusion—who seeks confirmation of his identity by looking through his things as he is taking a shower, whereas Pearl (after some initial disbelief) accepts his statements as true and Eve seems indifferent to whether they are true or not. A further connection between Nancy/Ann and Mickey is established through dreams (a motif that appears in a number of Rudolph films). One scene cuts from Nancy/Ann in bed to a dream scene, ending with a gun being fired, to a shot of Mickey waking up, leaving unanswered the question of whose dream was being presented. A variation on the scene is provided later when a shot of Zack firing a gun at a retreating Mickey is followed by a cut to Nancy/Ann sitting upright in bed. Guns and the potential for violence establish a bond between Mickey and Eve at the end of the film, when each threatens suicide as a means of forcing a commitment from the other.

If Nancy/Ann undergoes a kind of awakening, Eve can be seen to undergo a rebirth. She becomes an extension of the original Eve, who died (allegedly shooting herself over some guy—perhaps

Aspiring poet Pearl (Rae Dawn Chong) and possible pathological liar Mickey (Keith Carradine) meet in the "green world" of Eve's lounge. Courtesy Museum of Modern Art/Film Stills Archive.

Mickey?) and to whom Mickey believes he is returning when he first enters the bar. His desire to know this newfound Eve is demonstrated by his request to see more of her, "privately." His attentions bring about Eve's questioning of her belief that she is incapable of sustaining a marriage. This self-reflection takes a different form than that of Nancy/Ann, however. After Mickey has left the bar the second time, Eve walks forward toward the camera, indicating that, unlike Nancy/Ann, whom the camera seeks to penetrate by tracking in, Eve must be the instigator of her self-exploration.

Eve's rebirth is made complete when, at the end of the film, she finds herself in a position identical to that of the film's first Eve, threatening to shoot herself. Mickey calls her bluff, à la Spencer Tracy with the licorice gun in *Adam's Rib,* by threatening to do the same, and she realizes the depth of her concern for him and for their relationship. The fact that both Eve and Mickey claim to have unloaded guns during this scene is evidence of the bond between them, and the concept is reinforced when she tells him, "Who do you think you are, lying to me all the time? You are no better than I am. You and me are just the same."

If the working out of the relationship between Eve and Mickey has direct parallels with the comedies of remarriage, the remarriage concept is reinforced through other relationships as well, most notably that of Zack and Pearl. At one point, after Zack has beaten her, Pearl calls Nancy on the air. During the course of their conversation Pearl comments, "That's why I married him. Sex was all we had in common. . . . It was great. Then we started talking and it stopped working." This speech encapsulates the central conflict in the film between sexual fulfillment and emotional commitment. Pearl also speaks of "that feeling you have for a man that goes away," and, unlike the remarriage comedies, we are never provided with any clear evidence that the feeling returns, although Pearl does confront Eve at one point to tell her to keep away from her husband. Zack echoes the lack of knowingness in their relationship when he confides to Nancy/Ann, "You're the first person in years who's understood me." Nevertheless, Nancy/Ann retains her position as an unknown woman, and Zack's interaction with her, like his relationship with Pearl, is never fully resolved.

The one resolution we do get is between Eve and Mickey. Echoes of the remarriage comedy are apparent not just in the bus motif but in a reference to marriage as a form of gambling—a comment that equates Eve with her cinematic predecessor in *The Lady Eve.* A sense of "growing up together" is also suggested in Eve's observation that she has been planning the wedding "all my life," which negates her earlier observations about marriage. The bus setting indicates, however, that this relationship is not at a stopping point (even *It Happened One Night* ended at a fixed location) but is a journey just beginning. Thus the concept of remarriage becomes the basis for a new marriage, suggesting a circular rather than a linear progression. The bus motif also, of course, recalls the ending of Mike Nichols's *The Graduate* (1967), and Rudolph is equally enigmatic in his closing shot: he stays on a tight two-shot of Eve and Mickey, who have cryptic expressions on their faces, particularly Eve. Then, just as the film is fading, the camera subtly pans over toward Eve as she turns away from Mickey and smiles.

This ending provides a more positive indication of the potential for romanticism than do Rudolph's earlier works. The characters in *Welcome to L.A.* are unable to escape and, with the exception of Carroll, revert back to familiar patterns. Emily in *Remember My Name* is able to escape her past only by bringing closure to a relationship and by asserting her independence. In *Choose Me* Eve finds a way to escape and still sustain a relationship (though it is questionable how great an escape this will be, as she and Mickey's destination is Las Vegas, a place that epitomizes the neon-lit, artificial environment they have just left). Even Nancy/Ann, while asserting her independence, acknowledges that she is still learning about relationships between men and women, indicating that her process of self-discovery will continue.

Yet even with this apparent positivism, Rudolph emphasizes the external factors that act on contemporary relationships. All of the characters are initially faced with obstacles that prevent them from successful interactions, and all seek assistance from outside sources. Eve and Pearl both attempt to get reassurance from Dr. Love, who acknowledges that she has to be careful not to take her own advice too seriously. Mickey's willingness to marry every woman he meets becomes a form of noncommitment. Eve has developed a block against marriage because of her troubled past, while Pearl is stuck in a troubled present. She is beaten by Zack but justifies the action by indicating to Dr. Love during one of their phone conversations that at least he cares enough to hurt her (Pearl is wearing dark glasses to hide her black eye while talking to Dr. Love, a concept that will be associated in later Rudolph films with disintegrating relationships). Zack offers the only evidence in the film of an external power structure (although, interestingly, he is also acknowledged as a foreigner,

and the poker games he attends consist of an odd mixture of nation-
alities). Zack's relationships with Eve and Pearl are based on power
and possession (a trait that will become more pronounced in such
later Rudolph characters as Bertram Stone in *The Moderns*), while, by
contrast, Mickey claims his wives own him and that "it's everyone
else that breaks you up. Governments, cops, hospitals." Ironically,
Zack claims that Nancy/Ann, the one person he cannot possess or
control, is the one who understands him.

In addition to their seeking reassurance from Dr. Love, the characters view relationships in ways that are influenced by the processed
romanticism of popular culture. This is most directly implied in the
movie posters that decorate Pearl's apartment. Mickey first enters her
rooms, framed against a poster for *Don't Bother to Knock,* and makes
love to Pearl while an *All about Eve* poster "watches" from the edges
of the frame. Other posters (many of which are from film noir and
women's melodrama) include *The Accused* (featured prominently
when Zack catches Mickey taking pictures of Pearl in bed), *When
Ladies Meet, The Women,* and *Lady in the Dark* (the latter foreshadowing a moment later in the film when Mickey tells Eve, "You're not
alone in the dark"). When Pearl, under an assumed name, calls Dr.
Love and talks about her failed marriage with Zack, the posters
behind her provide ironic comment, from *Primrose Path* to the appropriately juxtaposed *The Man I Love* and *The Man I Married.* After she
hangs up, she examines her eye in the mirror next to a poster for *Too
Late for Tears.* A less direct allusion to past films is provided by the
placement in Eve's lounge of a Terry Chevillat painting of a trap
drum set that also formed a major part of the mise-en-scène in the
last scene of *Welcome to L.A.* (in which two women, Karen and
Linda, discuss the masks they have adopted). In contrast to the
movie-made romanticism of Pearl's apartment, the mise-en-scène of
Eve's house indicates violence as an aspect of popular culture by the
prominent placement of a Susan Scott painting that depicts a young
girl in a white dress stabbing a man with a knife (to which Rudolph
cuts at one point while Eve and Nancy/Ann are discussing marriage). The artwork in Eve's home also reinforces the unknown
woman concept through a painting that depicts a solitary woman.

Despite suggestions of darker forces, *Choose Me* is more intentionally
comedic than *Welcome to L.A.* or *Remember My Name.* From Pearl's
overripe poetry ("I'm not afraid of death / At least you get laid in your
coffin") to the dialogue exchanges between her and Mickey in the bar,
the script is filled with quotable comic dialogue. The classic farce structure is reinforced through the use of repetition and variation, particu-

larly in Zack's recurring confrontations with Mickey after finding him with each of the three female characters. The tightly constructed script culminates in a Preston Sturges–style dialogue exchange between Mickey and Eve in which each talks at cross-purposes, with Mickey assuming Eve is upset because he slept with Nancy/Ann, while she is actually accusing him of giving Pearl a black eye.

These farcical situations are played out in an atmosphere of artificially lit nightscapes, like a Feydeau farce in pink neon. In his earlier films Rudolph seemed to be striving for a means of displaying his characters' emotional states as well as their physical environment. With *Choose Me,* he and cinematographer Jan Kiesser achieve that effect, and it is the unique look of the film that has drawn the attention of many critics. The artificial neon lighting perfectly captures the film's mood, its pink and blue color schemes reflecting the potential romance but also the possibility of unrequited love. The opening scene captures a spontaneous sense of joy, as characters spill out onto the street from various clubs, including Eve's bar, and dance. They are presented in a flowing style that captures the feeling of a musical from Hollywood's golden age. Rather than the atmosphere of hesitancy and despair evoked by Richard Baskin's songs or the bluesy assertions of independence provided by Alberta Hunter, the Greek chorus-like songs of Teddy Pendergrass whisper hushed and erotic encouragements to the romantic couples.

Whereas night in *Welcome to L.A.* seems to emphasize the alienation and lonely desperation of the characters and in *Remember My Name* carries with it the potential for violence and nightmares from the past, in *Choose Me* it brings the characters to life. Rudolph has said that "nighttime is the most magical moment, the most romantic part of the day. Darkness is a dream and you do not wake up from it" (Garel, 81). The creation of a dreamlike atmosphere establishes an unreal quality, and Rudolph has suggested that the film's lack of a sense of physical reality allows for more focus on the truth of the emotional reality. It is this quality that has most often been singled out by supporters of the film as the element that makes it special. Night envelops the characters in a private world—a world in which the dangers of outside reality are forgotten. While the night also harbors the powers represented by Zack and his associates, these forces seem far removed from the intimacy of Eve's lounge. These powers, however, will take precedence in Rudolph's next film, *Trouble in Mind,* and while the characters still have the potential to escape or redefine themselves, their transformations come at a much higher price.

CHAPTER 5

Trouble in Mind:
Somewhere between Bogie
and Bowie

Everywhere there's rain, my love
Everywhere there's fear.
> —Tim Buckley, "Phantasmagoria in Two" (1967)

As much as *Choose Me* seemed to excite critics, *Trouble in Mind* (1986) appeared to alienate them. While the film received some strong notices and a few critics, including Roger Ebert, numbered it among the best of the year, many were unsure whether Rudolph intended the film as a serious revision of film noir or a parody of the genre. Although there are comic elements in the film (such as the increasingly odd appearance of Keith Carradine's character), they tend to grow out of the absurdity of the situations, whereas the humor in *Choose Me* grew out of the honesty of the characters. *Trouble in Mind* is in many ways the flip side of *Choose Me* (the title was actually inspired by a song in the earlier film), demonstrating the dangers of responding to the outside forces that hovered on the periphery of the previous film.

Although it anticipates a whole cycle of later new-wave noir films (producer Carolyn Pfeiffer described it as existing somewhere between Bogie and Bowie), *Trouble in Mind* also serves as a summation of Rudolph's work to date. In fact, its most characteristic romantic and noir elements have actually occurred before the film begins. A past relationship between the cop Hawk (Kris Kristofferson) and the café owner Wanda (Genevieve Bujold) has resulted in Hawk killing a man to protect her and being sent to prison. The romantic relationship between the innocent Georgia (Lori Singer) and her husband, Coop (Keith Carradine), has also been established prior to the outset of the film, and their marriage is already starting to disintegrate as the story begins. These events may be a product of the past or perhaps of the present, as Rudolph's Rain City appears to be a vaguely futuristic environment in which the efforts of these characters to come to terms with their previous existences result in either destruction or escape.

Like his hero Hawk, who re-creates the film's urban setting in miniature, Rudolph has manufactured a vaguely familiar but unsettlingly unreal world and has peopled it with characters who might have wandered in from his earlier films. In part, this feeling is generated by the performers themselves, who bring with them character associations from previous works. Hawk is played by Kris Kristofferson, fresh from the film *Songwriter* (1985), who expands on his dark-garbed loner image. Coop is played by Keith Carradine, going a step further from his *Choose Me* role in creating an enigmatic character who is trying to determine his own identity. Genevieve Bujold also extends her *Choose Me* character as an unknown woman who philosophizes about relationships but demands them on her own terms. Even those players new to the company carry associations to previous Rudolph characters. Lori Singer's wide-eyed innocent recalls the naive Lola and Travis of *Roadie* (1980) or the free-spirited housekeeper Linda in *Welcome to L.A.* (whose innocence was established by her seeming refusal to recognize her manipulation of or by men). The poet Solo (Joe Morton) could be a spiritual brother to Pearl in *Choose Me,* although he is an instigator of violence rather than a recipient of it. The other major character, Hilly Blue (Divine), foreshadows later Rudolph businessmen who subvert art for their own purposes (Hilly's house is actually the Seattle Art Museum, and the party he holds there degenerates into chaotic violence, resulting in the destruction of several works of art). Interestingly, the two male leads are generally referred to by abbreviated last names—Hawk for Johnny Hawkins and Coop for Billy Cooper—and the two female leads by their first names, while the androgynous Hilly Blue is often called by his full name (although Hawk, presumably in a contemptuous reflection on Hilly's lack of masculinity, refers to him only by his first name).

Supporting the noir atmosphere of the visual style, with its contrast of light and dark, is the musical score by Mark Isham. Rudolph has consistently used music in his films to create specific impressions, and it has often played a vital role in the construction of the films themselves. With Isham, Rudolph has found a musical collaborator who gives his films a consistency that becomes a key element in establishing a personal vision. Rudolph's private universe now not only has a look, but it also has a recognizable sound, and Isham's contributions bring unity even to less personal works, such as *Mortal Thoughts* (1991) and *Made in Heaven* (1987).

As in *Remember My Name,* the film begins with a character being released from prison, and it continues to reinforce the concept of entrapment and the need for characters to re-create themselves in order to escape from their private traps. Released from his cage, Hawk heads to Wanda's Café (a seedy version of Eve's lounge) to try to reconstruct his relationship with Wanda. But unlike Rudolph's earlier films—which offered at least the possibility of remarriage—here Wanda makes it immediately clear to "Johnny" (a name only she calls Hawk, suggesting a shared secret from their past) that she has finished her relationship with him and that what she has now is private. Hawk responds to her declaration of independence with violence, because he seeks to possess her. She later warns him never to cross that line again.

Coop and Georgia present a parallel relationship. While Hawk tries to reconcile with Wanda, Coop and Georgia grow further apart. As with Wanda and Hawk, their potential remarriage will be subverted, ironically because Coop's identity crisis takes him too far from where he started. The obvious bird imagery associated with their names defines their positions, with Hawk ultimately learning to fly, while Coop remains trapped. Coop's fate is established from the start when he misses out on a construction job and is told, "You're the early bird that didn't get the worm." His decision to rob the office of the construction company leads to his and Georgia's flight to Rain City, where Georgia takes a job at Wanda's while Coop looks for work. The city becomes another cage that finds Coop even more trapped, particularly after he is taken under the wing of the poet Solo, who quickly leads him into a life of crime. Although Solo claims he never uses guns, he produces one during the first job he and Coop do together. Later, when Solo comes to get Coop for another job, Rudolph positions Solo in the café between Coop and Georgia, who is holding their baby, establishing the poet as the force dividing the family unit.

Solo becomes representative of a society in which corruption, even disguised as poetry, becomes a seductive power that threatens family stability and real emotion. Just as Solo does for Coop, Rain City itself offers "a promise of something better," but instead becomes a corrosive force. Unlike the vacuous landscape of *Welcome to L.A.* or the dreamlike neon world of *Choose Me,* the environment of Rain City seems constantly claustrophobic and oppressive, with the gray days not all that distinguishable from the shadow-filled nights. When Coop and Georgia first arrive, a parade made up of militia men and grotesque clowns fills the streets, and the skies seem perpetually overcast. The location also seems to be inhabited by a diverse mix of cultures (at one point bagpipes are heard in the streets, and Solo seems to be into Oriental mysticism), and it is clear that the town is dominated by criminal elements.

Coop has already demonstrated his criminal tendencies by committing robbery, but this was an action motivated by anger, financial necessity, and revenge. Once he enters Rain City, however, he begins to lose his sense of identity, and his displacement is demonstrated visually by his increasingly exotic appearance. As his hair styles become progressively punk, a single lock of hair across his forehead undergoes modification until it takes the shape of a question mark, representing his complete lack of self-understanding. Once again Rudolph uses mirrors as a motif, associating them with Coop's self-reflection and search for identity as he descends into corruption. Fittingly, near the end of the film, when Georgia finds Coop in a hotel room with two prostitutes, the scene is filmed in a mirror, forcing Coop to reflect on what he has lost; he tries to chase after Georgia, but she tells him, "You can't even see what's happened, can you?"

Coop's increasingly androgynous appearance suggests that his loss of identity may owe in part to a sense of sexual confusion as he goes from a traditional family environment with Georgia and their child to consorting with male companions and attempting to reaffirm his heterosexual identity through liaisons with prostitutes. His androgyny is paralleled by the casting of transvestite Divine in the nondrag role of Hilly Blue. If Coop's coif becomes a reflection of his search for identity, Hilly's baldness suggests an emasculated state, and his need for power and control appears to stem from a lack of affection from his mother (Hilly comments dryly that he had to put her out of her misery). While more than one critic has identified the character as performing the function of Sydney Greenstreet in past noir works, Rudolph's casting of Divine (in addition to demonstrating the director's own quirky variations on genre conventions) clearly draws on the audience's familiarity with the performer's established screen image. One might be tempted to conclude that it is the androgynous characters who come to the worst ends in the film, with Coop losing Georgia and Hilly getting shot. Rudolph does not, however, seem to be suggesting an opposition to the lifestyle itself but to the dangers of denying one's own nature. Coop's self-destruction is brought about not by his androgyny but by his loss of awareness of who he is, and by appearing out of drag Divine denies his established screen image and his character pays the price.

Although he is warned by Solo when they first meet that "greed, like fire, transforms," Coop insists that he is not greedy and just wants to make some money. Nevertheless, Coop's tendency to target the wealthy and powerful at once positions him as being opposed to the affluent, wealth-obsessed social structure of the 1980s, as well as being a victim of it. The association of wealth with violence inevitably leads to destruction and becomes Rudolph's comment on the unavoidable path of the decade's economic climate. Coop's motivations for his criminal actions become unclear and seem to be generated by a general rebellion against a society that he feels has oppressed him—a rebellion that is made manifest in a violent opposition to all authority. It is only after Hilly, who appears to represent the major power in Rain City, is destroyed that Coop is able to reestablish some sense of himself and escape from his criminal life, walking calmly out of Hilly's house as apocalyptic chaos continues around him. Coop attempts to reconcile with Georgia, but his loss of identity has also left her with no sense of who he is, and she tells him she feels safer with Hawk. Coop reasserts his masculinity by joining the military (which presumably will make a man out of him again), and as he sits in a jeep in the rain waiting to be transported out of the city, he wipes the last vestiges of androgynous makeup from his face.

It might at first appear to us that Coop's descent into crime will be paralleled by Hawk's. A former cop who has served time after shooting a crime boss (and had found that the department would not condone his actions), Hawk tries to get back his job on the force after his release from prison. He gets angry when his boss turns him down and threatens to go over to the other side. Still, Hawk's sense of self is stronger than Coop's. Hawk maintains a personal code, and his acts of violence toward men are not committed out of revenge but in the defense of women. The initial shooting of the crime boss Fat Adolph was done to protect Wanda and is paralleled by the shooting of Hilly, which is done to help Georgia, as Hilly is planning to kill Coop.

If Hawk's violence toward men takes the form of destructive action, his violence toward women is manifested in sexual aggression. When he first returns to Wanda and she refuses to renegotiate their relationship, he takes her by force, while Georgia watches their shadows on the wall through the window of her trailer. Later, after Georgia has left her baby in the car of an "average" family and then has second thoughts and tries to get the child back, she calls on Hawk for help. Hawk tells her it will cost her and implies that the price will be her sexual submission to him. When she arrives at his room with a cake after he returns her baby, he sends her away but demands that they go to dinner together the next night. Demonstrating that she has begun to learn from Wanda how to demand love on her own terms, Georgia informs him that she might do that because she wants to, not because he is forcing her.

As Coop begins to lose his identity, Georgia seems to find hers. Like Emily in *Remember My Name,* she is reflected in a mirror as she tries on new clothes before her date with Hawk. Hawk has already been associated with Emily through the opening prison scene, and connections between Hawk and Georgia are made throughout the film. Hawk is reconstructing the city in miniature, and at one point, as he is working on his model, he looks out the window toward the trailer where Georgia is inside making paper dolls. He later tells her he thinks they have something in common. Although he does not elaborate, their common connection is that each is involved in a relationship with a partner who has gone beyond him or her in a way neither can understand. Even in the restaurant where they finally go for dinner, the concept of parallelism is reinforced, as their waitress identifies a club singer (who performs the film's title song) as her twin sister. Wanda later tries to convince Hawk that he should leave Georgia and start over, telling him, "Thank God love is blind, otherwise it'd see too much. You and her, you're missing so much. Shit, between the two of you there's almost a whole person."

The line anticipates the twin brothers in *Equinox* (1993), and like that film *Trouble in Mind* plays on contrasts between light and dark. The blond, angelic Georgia becomes the positive side of the dark, black-clad Hawk and also forms a contrast to the dark-haired Wanda. Wanda, in turn, has a single lock of hair that hangs down across her forehead and, though not as pronounced as Coop's question mark, connects the two characters, suggesting that her independence has brought with it a need for self-examination. Like Hawk, Wanda must learn to move from the world of the dark to the world of the light. Near the end of the film (after she has put her café up for sale) she tells Georgia that the reason she opened a morning café was because it was the best place to watch the sun rise. Although Wanda's fate is left unresolved at the end of the film, her past association with Hawk implies that his escape, indicated in the final shot of him driving away from the dark city while the sun breaks through the clouds (a shot that, interestingly, recalls the ending of *Blade Runner* [1982], another futuristic film noir), also becomes a form of release for her.

The focus on Hawk at the beginning and end of the film indicates that the film is his journey—from the time he is released from his cage until he finds, as Marianne Faithfull sings over the closing credits, his "Freedom to Fly." Of course, as is the case with characters in other Rudolph films, Hawk can only achieve that freedom after paying off old debts. His attempt to reestablish his relationship with Wanda leads to an understanding of her own right to freedom, and his conflicts with Coop and Hilly force him to come to terms with his own violent nature. Wanda becomes his conscience (even though he tells her, "You can't live on philosophy"), and it is his past relationship with her that eventually helps him to understand why his present relationship with Georgia cannot survive. Coop and Georgia, whose arrival in the city coincides with Hawk's release from prison, represent the two extremes his future might take. Georgia offers the possibility of home and security, while Coop represents the potential for violence. Although not taken to the spiritual level of later films (except, perhaps, in the final dream image of Georgia briefly appearing beside Hawk in the car as he takes flight), these characters are representative of the struggle between darkness and light, or violence and redemption, which is the essence of Rudolph's worldview. Hawk's re-creation of the city in miniature might even be taken on a metaphysical level to suggest that the other characters do not actually exist, that they are the manifestations of Hawk's attempt to come to terms with different aspects of his identity—a concept emphasized in shots in which views of the miniature city are intercut with those of the "real" one.

Inevitably, violence becomes intertwined with romance, quite literally, as Hawk's relationship with Georgia is intercut with the misguided attempt by Coop and Solo to hold up a businessman and his child bride. Although the interlude with Hawk and Georgia ends with a kiss, the next day at the café he treats her cruelly when she waits on him. Coop's arrival at the café escalates into violence, built up in a series of quick cuts as Coop knocks a guy over when he throws open the door (repeating an earlier action in the film), and Georgia drops the plates she is carrying to Hawk. It is Wanda who finally gets control of the gun, driving Coop and Solo out.

After Georgia confronts Coop in the hotel room, she runs out into the street and is stopped by Hawk. Georgia and Hawk return to Hawk's room. Although Georgia realizes the impossibility of continuing a relationship with Coop, she asks Hawk to help get him out of trouble, and Hawk agrees on the condition that, once he sends Coop on his way, she will belong to him (once again confusing love with ownership and possession). He adds that he will live with her and take care of her kid, suggesting his desire for a domestic life. When Hawk and Georgia eventually consummate their relationship, Rudolph cuts from a lengthy shot of the two of them kissing to a shot of them in bed reflected in a mirror with an odd geometric shape, implying an asymmetrical quality to their association, as though each has found in the relationship some further sense of his or her identity but have not achieved a "well-rounded" image of the normal family life that Hawk is seeking.

Hawk's connection with violence and romance confirms his role as both film noir and romantic comedy hero. His name might even be taken as an homage to Howard Hawks, a director who worked with equal success in both genres. While Hawk's association with Georgia and Wanda develops along the lines of romantic comedy (though admittedly with a darker edge), his confrontation with corrupt forces follows the noir pattern. There is a familiarity to the story of a cop who served time and now finds himself on the outs with the system of which he was once a part and who finds he has to act on his own to oppose corruption. The difference in Rudolph's film comes not in the plot itself but in the motivations, as Hawk's opposition to the underworld grows not because of a sense of doing what is right but because of his commitment to helping Georgia. Hawk, in fact, makes little effort to go after the major players in the underworld until the end of the film. Much of his violence prior to the finale is directed at Coop and is a product of jealousy rather than an attempt to keep Coop from entering a life of crime. Hawk, in fact, seems for much of the film to be the discoverer of violence rather than the instigator of it, as in the scene in which he finds that Solo has been drowned inside his own car (making good, at least partially, Hilly's threat that he would have Coop's and Solo's lungs filled with water).

Yet Hawk's commitment to Georgia becomes a form of ownership, and this is what finally dooms their relationship. This becomes a symptom of the city itself, in which possession becomes a motivating force. Most of the characters are not seeking the shared responsibility of a romantic relationship but rather control. Some, such as Wanda, seek control of their own lives, while others, especially Hilly, seek control of the lives of others. In a move toward the principal theme in *The Moderns,* a part of that control is equated with art and artifacts. As I indicated earlier, Hawk's construction of a miniature city may be a form of reconstructing his own identity. His artistic endeavor is paralleled by Georgia's more naive (in keeping with her innocent nature) construction of paper dolls and Wanda's collection of statues, which she implies are endowed with spiritual powers. These objects become associated with the identity of each character and, unlike Hilly's artworks, are meant to be examined and contemplated rather than merely owned. Hawk's final confrontation with Hilly makes him realize the inadequacy of possession without love. While Hawk confuses the two, Hilly has substituted one for the other and expresses a general contempt for women. It is this issue of control, whether of art or of people, that Rudolph suggests is the greatest danger of modern society and can lead to denial of genuine emotions.

Hawk's confrontation with Hilly ends with a chaotic, absurdist vision of a destructive society—a society in which everyone seems to own a gun and where even the violence is an emotionless response. This finale became the point of contention for many critics, who were unsure as to whether Rudolph intended it to be an excessive parody or a serious statement. To a director who admits to viewing society—particularly American society—as unreal and absurd, it is quite likely that he intended it to be both. Rudolph acknowledged this characteristic in discussing *Trouble in Mind:*

> Once I realized I was going to take the leap with Divine, this was not going to be a conventional film. When Keith got involved we started talking about how this guy should go through these transformations. I never realized we would take it to such an exaggerated level, but then it seemed to be the way to do the story without taking it totally seriously. If you do these retro story plot ideas and take them terribly seri-

ously, then you've made another exercise. The times seemed to be going through that culturally, with Reagan and all that; it just seemed to be an unfamiliar terrain that we were living in. There was an absurdity to the whole film that I kind of enjoyed—people talking funny languages, all the gangsters were inarticulate people who don't even use words so they just growl. . . . What it really is is this thing that gets me in trouble all the time, which is this simultaneous serious-humorous. If you ask me to make a film that is the most accurate reflection that you see of our condition right now, I'd make a version of *Trouble in Mind* or *Equinox*. I see it—it's *absurd*. (Smith, 71)

CHAPTER 6

The Moderns: Art Is Only an Infection; Some People Get It and Some People Don't

We know that Art is not truth. Art is a lie that makes us realize truth, at least the truth that is given us to understand. The artist must know the manner whereby to convince others of the truthfulness of his lies.

—Pablo Picasso, "Picasso Speaks" (1923)

While Rudolph was in Cannes in 1982 to promote the release of *Return Engagement* (1983), he reportedly caused some comment by refusing to allow an interviewer to reuse a tape on which the reporter had previously interviewed Martin Scorsese. As Rudolph explained, "I didn't know the ground rules that everything is disposable, including your last good idea. . . . I just thought it was wrong to destroy originals. It was a document of a one-time event."[1] It is fitting that when the director returned, cinematically, to France (albeit by way of Montreal) in his film *The Moderns* (released in 1988), he would deal with the issue of what constitutes art in a disposable society. In the film's most audacious scene, a wealthy businessman destroys masterworks of Matisse, Modigliani, and Cézanne because he believes they are forgeries and have no monetary value.

The script for *The Moderns* was written after Rudolph made *Welcome to L.A.,* and there are clear similarities to that film in both its ensemble story and in its consideration of deception, which in this case is explored not just in terms of romantic pursuits but also in relation to artistic endeavors. There is even a suggestion of a conflict between the lead character, again played by Keith Carradine, and his father—a theme that Rudolph has seldom addressed in his later works. The final version of *The Moderns,* however, also incorporates themes that Rudolph gradually had been developing in his work during the decade it took for the film to be made. The equation of artistic pursuit with the search for personal identity can be traced back to *Welcome to L.A.* and became a central concern of *Made in Heaven,* the film Rudolph made just prior to *The Moderns.* In *Welcome to L.A.,* however, there is little sense of the outside forces acting on the artist (the producers of the album are not identified, and the manipulation that has brought Carroll to Los Angeles was not an attempt to control him artistically but to bring about a reconciliation between father and son). The issue of control and ownership that surfaces in *Trouble in Mind* becomes a key consideration in *The Moderns.*

The film once again involves a central triangular relationship with other relationships presented as offshoots. Here, however, the goal of many of the characters is more than just a successful romantic relationship. They are driven by a desire for control, and Rudolph explores the manner in which they not only deceive themselves and each other, but also the ways in which they manipulate one another to achieve their own ends. Art becomes a major factor in these manipulations, and thus the exploration of these relationships reflects not only on human interaction but also on how artistic value is defined in a commercial society.

The basic plot concerns Nick Hart (Keith Carradine), who has artistic aspirations but works in Paris as a cartoonist for an American paper. Like Humphrey Bogart in the 1942 film *Casablanca* (who told his lover, "We'll always have Paris"), Hart finds his life complicated by the return of a lover, in this case his former wife, Rachel (Linda Fiorentino). Rachel shows up at one of Hart's watering holes in the company of her new husband, Bertram Stone (John Lone), a wealthy businessman who is investing in art. While dealing with this triangular situation, Hart, whose father was a successful art forger, is also faced with a dilemma of artistic integrity when he is asked to copy three paintings for Nathalie de Ville (Geraldine Chaplin), because she is leaving her husband and wants to take the original paintings with her. Although Hart is at first reluctant, he responds to the challenge of trying to reproduce successfully the style of three master artists, and he makes the copies. After Nathalie's husband dies, she decides she no longer needs Hart's services, and when he insists that she stick to their agreement, she attempts to steal back the original paintings from his studio, but she gets the copies instead. Hart sells the originals to his dealer, Libby Valentin (Genevieve Bujold), who in turn sells them to Stone. When Nathalie arrives at the opening of Stone's exhibition and denounces the paintings as fakes, insisting that she has the originals, Stone destroys the paintings. The conflict between Hart and Stone over Rachel erupts in violence, and after Rachel leaves both of them, Stone commits suicide. Hart leaves for America with columnist Oiseau (Wallace Shawn), who has faked his own death to get out of his contract with the newspaper for which he worked. At the Metropolitan Museum of Art in New York Hart discovers his forgeries are being hailed as masterpieces, and he is reunited with Rachel.

In *The Moderns* (1988), art collector Bertram Stone (John Lone) is confronted by Nathalie de Ville (Geraldine Chaplin) at a reception to exhibit Stone's latest acquisitions. After Nathalie implies that three of the works are fakes, Stone viciously destroys the priceless paintings.
Courtesy Museum of Modern Art/Film Stills Archive.

Rudolph employs this outline to create an environment in which individual creativity is packaged for mass consumption and art is used for commerical gain, personal control, or the manufacturing of myth. In summarizing the film, Rudolph observed that "what Paris meant to me—and I think this is true of our generation—is a place where modern painters, writers, and artists unwittingly carved out the ground rules of advertising, which is a kind of forgery of art, isn't it?" (Jaehne, 26). It is this aspect of the film that has been misunderstood by many critics, who accused the director of misrepresenting the period and evading the issue of what actually constitutes art. Rudolph is less concerned with an absolute definition of art than with how it is determined by others in society. Significantly, his characters are not established artists but hover on the edges of the artistic community, either as buyers (Stone), sellers (Libby), forgers (Hart), gossips (Oiseau), or sources of inspiration (Rachel). As Rudolph has stated, "*The Moderns* was always a film about the people at the other table; not the people at the A table" (Combs, 69). While not actually creating art (with the possible exception of Hart), the characters become influential in determining its worth. Libby and Stone establish market value, and Oiseau, who fancies himself on an equal level with the artists about whom he writes, uses his influence as a critic to dictate artistic value to the masses. As he proudly observes to Hart during his fake funeral, "If it weren't for me, people would have thought surreal was a breakfast food."

Even the actual members of the Lost Generation (presumably "the A table") encountered through these characters seem not to contribute to art itself as much as to the manufacturing of an image of what constitutes art. Gertrude Stein, for example, is briefly glimpsed in the salon where she holds court for an entourage of adoring admirers. After being told that Hart is 33, she cavalierly announces that "American painters are 26 this year." Her pronouncement has nothing to do with critical insight and everything to do with her belief in her own manufactured image as a caustic wit. Hart asserts his independence by telling her "Well, I'm not," and Stein acidly responds, "Precisely my point. Then you won't fit in at all." Apparently lost on her is the irony of imposing conformity on a form of personal expression.

In a more pronounced role, Hemingway (Kevin J. O'Connor) appears as a more disheveled version of one of Rudolph's poets and draws on the experiences of Hart and his associates as material for his work. The Hemingway image itself has not been completely defined, as indicated by a brief shot of two tourists mistaking him for F. Scott

Fitzgerald, and he seems to have difficulty getting the details right (at one point, as he muses over variations on his "Moveable Feast" metaphor, Oiseau casually informs him, "I'd work on that"). Yet it is Hemingway who gives perhaps the nearest insight into the artistic process, as he begins reshaping events, almost as soon as they happen, into the raw material for his work, gradually confusing the names of the real people with those of his fictional creations. Echoing the suggestion that the characters in *Trouble in Mind* may have been created by Hawk to inhabit his miniature city, Rudolph has indicated in *The Moderns* that "Hemingway might be creating this whole thing as it happens" (Combs, 69). Even the name of the protagonist recalls Hemingway's hero Nick Adams (as well as the narrator of F. Scott Fitzgerald's *The Great Gatsby,* another story in which a man attempts to use wealth and power to achieve romantic fulfillment).

Aside from Hemingway, the one principal character who appears to possess a degree of artistic integrity is Hart. Although he is a forger, he takes artistic pride in the creation of his copies. Like Hemingway, he also sees art as a means by which to reinvent reality. Even while making his forgeries, he incorporates an image of Rachel into the face of a Modigliani nude, adding his personal touch to what is essentially an imitation. As Eva Rueschmann suggests in "Desire and Loss in Alan Rudolph's *The Moderns,*" the incorporation of Rachel's image establishes a connection between Hart's desire for her and his act of forgery.[2] The incident might be taken to further imply that their love is a kind of forgery, once again reinforcing the equation in Rudolph's work between love and deception. Given his artistic abilities, Hart is presumably the character most likely to understand what really constitutes art, rather than what the public has been told to believe. Yet he, too, undermines the mystique of the artistic impulse when he describes how he got cold chills the first time he saw a Cézanne but then goes on to explain that it turned out to be pneumonia rather than artistic inspiration and that it was while he was recovering that he took up drawing.

Hart's undercutting of the spiritual nature of the artistic impulse and the less than traditional depiction of Papa Hemingway are indicative of Rudolph's myth-shattering view of the period—an approach that is appropriate to a film dealing with deception and the creation of image. In this respect, *The Moderns* has an obvious affinity to Altman's *Buffalo Bill and the Indians* in its implication that what has been accepted as history is really a myth manufactured for mass consumption. Rudolph has indicated that his tampering with the

Artist Nick Hart (Keith Carradine) incorporates the image of his former lover, Rachel, into a forgery he has been commissioned to paint.
Courtesy Film Center of Chicago.

accepted version of Paris in the 1920s was another aspect of the film that was misunderstood and that infuriated members of the art world. In an interview in *Sight and Sound,* Rudolph stated,

> Most people have approached [the film] as though it were intended to be a definitive history of the period. Yet, our whole recollection of that period is based on myth. It has been imagined and reimagined and packaged; our references are from memoirs and gossip and innuendo and lies. . . . I guess the problem some critics have had with the film is that they don't like their myths being replaced with other myths. Our intention was not to be factual or accurate, but to show some of these characters, Hemingway in particular, before the cement had dried on the statue.[3]

As if to reinforce the notion that what we are seeing should not be taken literally, Rudolph continually calls into question our perception of physical reality. On one level, the film itself is an elaborate deception, as Paris was re-created in Montreal. Although Rudolph does not call attention to the ruse (unlike his mentor Altman, who ended his film *Beyond Therapy* [1987] by demonstrating in the final shot that the alleged New York–based story had actually been filmed in Paris), there are deliberate indications throughout the film of an unreal environment. The opening shots establish a distortion of normal perspective and indicate the manner in which art is manufactured for mass consumption. Footage of the Eiffel Tower—viewed through a gate being opened by an attendant—quickly fades to another view of the tower—a miniature being carried on a tray to Hart's table at a café. Perhaps the most deliberate indication of an unreal perspective occurs in a scene in which Hart and Nathalie drive through the city (presented in a shot composition that recalls the ending scene of Henry King's film of *The Sun Also Rises* [1957]). Although the exteriors appear to be actual city streets, an oval window between Hart and Nathalie while they are in the back seat of a cab provides glimpses of exterior scenes that have the flat, distorted appearance of expressionistic paintings. When Oiseau and Hart decide to return to Hollywood ("where the pictures move"), Rudolph uses a painting of an ocean liner to depict their voyage. This deliberately artificial image recalls some of the later works of Federico Fellini (especially *Fellini's Casanova* [1976] and *And the Ship Sails On* [1983]), and, like Fellini, Rudolph employs such techniques as reminders that film itself is a modification of reality. Along with the use of artificial images that contradict out sense of space, Rudolph incorporates elements that suggest a defiance of our perceptions of time. At one point the camera pans across a bar inhabited by many of the principal characters and ends with a shot of patrons dressed in punk and new-wave styles of the 1980s. While some have criticized the shot for attempting to equate the Lost Generation of the 1920s with contemporary social deviants, it is more likely intended to reinforce the notion that art, in any period, is a matter of image, style, and personal expression.

The surrealist touches are extended to the character of Stone, who is seemingly the most materialistic and least artistically inclined of the characters. Early in the film a reference is made to Stone having been an assistant to Harry Houdini, setting up one of the film's most bizarre moments. The conflict between Stone and Hart over Rachel culminates in a highly stylized confrontation that ends with Stone committing suicide by falling into the river next to an abstract image of the Eiffel Tower. Hart recovers the body and places it in the coffin being prepared for Oiseau's funeral. During the burial service Stone, apparently seen only by Hart, rises from the grave and frees himself from a straitjacket, as though his suicide, the ultimate act of artistic self-indulgence, has freed him from his materialism and allowed his creative spirit to escape. The fact that only Hart seems to witness this rebirth confirms his ability to recognize art while those around him understand only image. Because the film takes place in 1926, the year Houdini died, Stone's resurrection might also be taken as the rebirth of the master magician, who had expressed a belief in the afterlife and vowed to return.

Prior to this surprisingly positive resurrection, Stone has been treated as a negative force. While others in the film use their influence to determine what will be seriously regarded as art, Stone equates art strictly with market value. His attitude is summed up in this observation about a painting: "If I paid less, it would be less beautiful." Later, at the opening of his exhibition, where Nathalie confronts him with the charge that three of his paintings are fakes, he says, "There's no value, except what I choose to put on it. This is art because I paid hard cash for it." When Natalie's charges are supported by supposed experts, Stone responds by mutilating the paintings. He throws the Matisse in the fire and cuts the nipple from a Modigliani nude (the face of which, we have earlier seen, resembled a photograph of his wife).

This latter action demonstrates not only Stone's attitude toward art but also toward women. Although the mutilation is an extreme act, the painting itself reflects the concept of objectification of the female form, and this concept extends to Stone's treatment of Rachel. Early in the film he establishes the connection between Rachel and one of his acquisitions when he refers to her as "a perfect work of art" and adds that "no painter has ever captured her beauty and probably never will." Hart sums up Stone's position when he tells Hemingway that Stone "thinks just because he buys something that he owns it. It's all the same to him. A piece of ass, a piece of property. It's all about ownership. He doesn't own me, he doesn't own Rachel and he never will."

Stone's attitudes are seemingly contrasted by those of Hart. Even their names have obvious metaphoric connotations, with Hart equated not only with "art" but also with a sense of passion, whereas Stone indicates something hard, rigid, and incapable of feeling. This contrast is demonstrated in two parallel scenes involving Rachel in a bathtub. In the first, Stone brutally sodomizes her while the camera remains on Rachel, indicating the pain she has endured. Later, Hart appears in the bathroom nude while she is bathing and prepares to make love, but she insists that they do so on the floor rather than in the tub. In addition to recalling her previous experience, this demand on her part demonstrates her ability to take control in her relationship with Hart.

Despite such contrasts, however, Hart also objectifies Rachel. When he first sees her in the café, Hart tells Oiseau he wants to make love to her and then paint her. Later, he actually manages to work her image into the Modigliani. For all their differences, parallels are established between Hart and Stone, indicating that each regards Rachel as something to be controlled rather than as a person to be treated as an equal. During a gathering at Gertrude Stein's parlor, Hart slaps Rachel when she laughs after Stone insults his art and his clothes. The action is echoed later, following Stone's humiliation during his disastrous exhibition opening, when he slaps a drunken Rachel because she tells him she feels sorry for him.

Hart's attack on Rachel at the salon causes Stone to demand retribution, and a boxing match is arranged (which Stone regards as "very American"). The bout encapsulates the battle waged by the two men for control of Rachel—a dominance that they feel can only be attained through brutality. Ironically, the boxing concept incorporates key motifs associated with their attempts to establish ownership of Rachel, as the arena consists of a ring (recalling the actual wedding of Hart and Rachel) and canvas (the painting concept).

Although Hart's attempts to win back Rachel would seem to contain elements of the remarriage pattern, Rachel maintains her status as an unknown (and unowned) woman throughout the film by reiterating her refusal to be treated like a possession. This position is established in the opening scene when Hemingway asks Hart if he knows her, and Hart responds, "I'm not sure that's possible." A short time later, when she meets Hart and they recall their past relationship, the issue of deception is connected to the concept of knowingness:

Hart: I don't trust you, Rachel. All the trust is gone.
Rachel: You hate me.
Hart: How can I hate someone I don't even know?
Rachel: You know me, Nicky.

Hart's comment on no longer trusting Rachel is echoed by Stone, who sarcastically observes, shortly before assaulting Rachel in the bathtub, "If you can't trust your wife, who can you trust?" Despite her insistence that Hart understands her, Rachel makes it clear that there is a distinction between knowing and owning. When she goes to visit Hart in his loft, she tells him, "You don't own me. Nobody owns me." She leaves her wedding ring behind as a gesture of her independence. The concept is reversed when she confronts Stone, who seemingly does own her (because, as she tells Hart, he knows how to take care of her). Although he insists, "I know everything about you," she responds, "You don't know anything about me."

This exchange occurs during the final confrontation between the two men, when Stone discovers that Hart and Rachel are still legally married. As in the finale of *Choose Me,* the romantic conflict erupts in violence, with the two men struggling over a gun. Rachel again asserts her independence by insisting, "I'll decide what happens to me." Like Eve, she asserts her control over her own life by holding the gun to her head. Rachel retains her independent status right up to the end, when she suddenly appears before Hart at the Metropolitan Museum of Art. As the two embrace, they block out the painting he had done in which he had incorporated her face, suggesting that their relationship will overcome his work, which appears to have been the source of their marital discord, as well as his objectification of her.

While Stone and Hart engage in a physical battle over Rachel, Stone also attempts to gain a psychological advantage by demonstrating the power of commerce over art (he has made his fortune in prophylactics, which humorously comments on his desire to control the process of creation). Following their boxing match, Stone suggests that he might be interested in purchasing some of Hart's work. Hart shows up at Stone's home claiming he did not bring any samples and stating that he does not want to be collected because it makes him feel like a manufacturer. He has actually hidden a painting in the entryway so he can pretend to go back to Libby's gallery while sneaking upstairs to see Rachel. The psychological battle continues when Hart "returns" with the painting and Stone attempts to belittle him by offering a low price, not realizing that Hart has just made love to Rachel. Stone's final victory occurs, however, when Hart's painting ends up being used as part of an advertisement for Stone's business enterprises.

Stone's obsession with the commercial value of art is paralleled in the motivations of Nathalie and Libby. Like Stone, Nathalie only appears to be interested in art as a means of gaining power in a relationship. As with Karen in *Welcome to L.A.,* however, she also seeks an idealized notion of romance. While trying to seduce Hart into forging her paintings, she tells him, "Don't confuse sex and love, Mr. Hart. It'll spoil both of them for you" (a statement that is paralleled by Rachel's observation that "there's a big difference between love and passion" when explaining to Hart why she left him for Stone). Nathalie also insists, "If you're in love with someone or something, you have to surrender to it." Perhaps it is her ability to separate sex and love that explains why she is willing to accept Hart's terms when he insists on something more than money from her.

Although Libby is less manipulative in her use of art, she is also more concerned with commercial gain than with artistry. She appears to recognize some ability in Hart's work, calling it "the shock of the new," but reminds him that the first principle of artistic survival is to parlay talent into cash. During her meeting with Stone about the purchase of Nathalie's paintings, their negotiations take on an almost erotic intensity. Like Stone, Libby tends to equate artistic value with commerical value (when Stone responds to his humiliation at the exhibition by destroying her gallery, she informs Hart that not only were his paintings slashed but also the "valuable ones").

Yet it is also Libby who suggests that artistic achievement may have little to do with critical assessment when she tells Hart, "I never liked Caravaggio myself, but your father's Caravaggio I loved." This suggestion that even deliberate deception might have artistic value seems a logical conclusion in a film in which notions of what constitutes art are largely a matter of imaging. Stone's evaluation of art based on how much he paid for it is probably no less ludicrous than the buyer who comes to Libby's gallery seeking something to go with his blue walls or the various critics and experts who insist (ironically and erroneously in the final scene) that art is something that can never be duplicated. Rudolph has identified the discussion raised by the film as "whether or not it makes any difference that a work is an original or a copy. And if it does make a difference, doesn't it lay with the people who can tell the difference? The film brings up the price that is paid, but then you've got to ask, is the value in the work itself or in the response to it?" (Jaehne, 29). Rudolph might be echoing the observations of Walter Benjamin, who in "The Work of Art in the Age of Mechanical Reproduction" discusses the transformation of emphasis from the cult value of art to its exhibition value. Benjamin acknowledges the role of photography and, by extension, of film in bringing about this transition—a conclusion that perhaps provides the motivation for Rudolph's implication throughout the film that Hollywood is becoming the focus of attention for Oiseau and (albeit more reluctantly) Hart.

The issue of the uniqueness of a work—its inability to be duplicated, which has often been used as a yardstick in measuring artistic achievement—seems even more tenuous in an age of mechanical reproductions, and it is appropriate that the characters reject the increasingly commercial and image-conscious Paris of the 1920s for the home of the one true "modern" mechanical art form, the motion picture. This was another element of the film that drew objections from critics, who suggested that it would make sense for the gossip columnist Oiseau to want to go to Hollywood, but not Hart. Yet one senses that Hart's exodus is motivated not so much by a passion for Hollywood as by a need for escape (bringing him to the point of so many of Rudolph's characters). He sees no future in an environment where artistic achievement has become less important than evaluations of it, where the Gertrude Steins can determine what is art for the masses, and, finally, where he believes he has lost Rachel, his source of inspiration.

It should also be noted that the setting in 1926 indicates a time when film was beginning to realize its artistic potential (this was, after all, only one year after the release of Eisenstein's *Potemkin*), when it was still possible to regard Hollywood as "the city of the future," although Hart reminds Oiseau that he said the same thing about Paris six years earlier and concludes that it would be more fun to watch the movies than to make them. In an age when the reception of art and the ability to present it to a mass audience was becoming an increasing concern, film represented the epitome of a form of expression that could reach the greatest number of people at one time. It is fitting that the one true twentieth-century art form should be an attraction to the characters in a film entitled *The Moderns*. As Rudolph noted, "Basically what the 1920s did, with art and fashion, was to announce to the world that we had entered the twentieth century. The artists had discovered it earlier through their work, machinery had discovered it through a war and war productivity, but the world in general discovered it in the 1920s, when art and commerce came together" (Trainor, 233). Ironically, Rudolph hints that the new medium of expression is already being subjected to the same kinds of outside influences that have altered the art world of Hart's Paris. During one scene in the Bar Selavy, Rudolph includes a shot of a critic who is extolling the virtues of film and pontificating that the impact of cinema will compel a total revolution of values.

Whether this revolution will be a positive or negative change is left unaddressed, but cinema certainly seems well suited to the merging of art and commerce—an amalgamation that Rudolph regards as the determining characteristic of this century. This assessment of cinema is also an appropriate statement from a director whose entire career seems to have reflected a conflict between artistic projects and commercial ones, particularly coming on the heels of *Made in Heaven* (1987), an especially frustrating experience in commercial filmmaking in which Rudolph's artistic vision was undermined by the studio's controlling forces.

CHAPTER 7

Love at Large: Searching for a Heart

Eve is a twofold mystery.
>   —Elizabeth Barrett Browning, *The Poet's Vow* (1836)

Love at Large (1991) is a perfect title for a film that merges elements of romantic comedy with the detective genre. The latter might suggest another film noir variation, and elements of the plot support such a reading, including a seeming femme fatale, bigamous relationships, and, as always, the potential for violence. The film seems closer in tone, however, to the goofy coincidental interactions and desperate romance of *Choose Me* than the darker undercurrents of *Trouble in Mind.* Also, whereas plot has often been at the service of character development in Rudolph's films, here characters are more at the service of plot, and the director seems less concerned with their private motivations than with the directions in which their quests lead them. Some characters (particularly those played by Barry Miller, Ruby Dee, and Kevin J. O'Connor) seem to be included mainly to provide additional complications for the narrative and are only sketchily developed.

Much of *Love at Large* seems like a structural exercise, designed to connect characters in ever-expanding variations of Rudolph's favorite geometric configuration—the triangle. The territory is mapped out in the opening images, beginning with a characteristic defocused shot that turns out to be the headlight of a bus. On the bus is a young couple wrapped in an embrace (perhaps suggesting that the film will pick up where *Choose Me* left off), and as the bus drives away it reveals another couple kissing on the sidewalk. This view of a world dominated by romance is accompanied by Leonard Cohen (a noir romantic if ever there was one) singing "Ain't No Cure for Love" on the soundtrack, which offers a counterbalance to the heady atmosphere by describing attraction in terms of addiction ("I've got you like a habit / And I'll never get enough"). This hint of something more dangerous existing beneath the surface foreshadows the rest of the scene, as the camera cranes up and into a partly opened window (in a shot that recalls the opening of Hitchcock's *Psycho*), ending on a photograph of a happy couple that is knocked over just as the camera closes in on it.

The individuals in the photograph are detective Harry Dobbs (Tom Berenger) and his girlfriend, Doris (Ann Magnuson), who at the moment are involved in a fierce argument instigated by Doris's jealousy over Harry's professional work, establishing a familiar triangle in which the male character's job is a source of friction in a relationship even before outside factors add tension. The third side of the triangle is about to take on a human dimension, as Harry receives a call from the mysterious Miss Dolan (Anne Archer), who offers him a job, sparking another burst of violent behavior from Doris. As Harry prepares to leave he searches for his gun and finds it wrapped in lace in a drawer—an image that neatly encapsualtes the film's genre crossbreeding.

Harry encounters Miss Dolan at a nightclub called the Blue Danube, which, like the client herself, seems to belong to another time. As if to emphasize that Harry (and by extension the viewer) will not be given a complete depiction of this enigmatic figure, Rudolph presents Miss Dolan in a series of fragmented images during their conversation, focusing on her hand as she spreads money out on the table, then on her lips as she sings a few lines from a song, and tilting up to her eyes when she pleads to Harry, "Please say yes." Rudolph also uses their initial encounter to establish a dialogue that plays like a parody of noir:

> Miss Dolan: They say you can be trusted.
> Harry: Who says I can be trusted?
> Miss Dolan: I saw it in a phone book at the train station.

Miss Dolan has hired Harry to track her lover, Rick, but before Harry can get additional information she kisses him and then leaves.

Spotting the man he believes to be his target, Harry follows him, and after various shots of his surveillance, the suspect returns home to his wife and kids. It is at this point that Rudolph begins to complicate the plot and introduce his ever-expanding series of triangles. In another Hitchcockian echo (the case of mistaken identity that leads so many Hitchcock heroes into chaos), the man being followed is not Rick but Fredrick King (Ted Levine), and although he is the wrong man as far as Harry's case is concerned, he also has a secret identity that has him caught in a romantic triangle. King is actually living a double life as James McGraw, a wealthy rancher with another wife and a daughter.

From this point, Rudolph works continual variations on the themes of deception and the search for romantic fulfillment. Mrs. McGraw (Kate Capshaw) also has a lover, a young ranch hand named Art (Kevin J. O'Connor), but their relationship exists in an atmosphere of guilt and deception because of the lie of her marriage to McGraw. As Harry begins to absorb all of that, reporting back to Miss Dolan in the belief that the bigamist is Rick, he is also being tailed by another detective, Stella (Elizabeth Perkins), who has been hired by the jealous Doris. Stella is seen at several points during Harry's surveillance of King/McGraw before her character is identified. During Harry's second meeting with Miss Dolan, Stella passes behind their table and then walks past Harry and gives him the eye after Miss Dolan leaves. At first this encounter seems to reinforce the random qualities implied at the outset of the film, and only later is it revealed that there is a deliberate purpose in her attention to Harry.

It is Stella who makes the most direct connection between the literal search for truth that is a defining feature of the detective genre and the more abstract search for love that motivates romantic comedy. While spying on Harry, she sits in her car and reads from *The Love Manual* (which could have been written by Dr. Nancy Love) and reveals her vulnerability at the times when she is trying to act toughest. Inevitably, she and Harry meet and further complicate the film's romantic entanglements. Stella is involved in a relationship and also claims dedication to her career (although we later discover that this is her first job and that she took it while "on the rebound from a bad love deal"), whereas Harry continues to maintain telephone contact with Doris and is clearly becoming increasingly fascinated by Miss Dolan. The connection between the two detectives is established in two shots, the first pulling back from Stella in her motel room after she talks to Doris on the phone, followed by a track in to

In *Love at Large* (1990), would-be detective Stella Wynkowski (Elizabeth Perkins) uses the occasion of a stakeout to contemplate the theory that "lovers are the ones who wait." Stella recalls other Rudolph heroines who seek advice from outside sources in trying to understand interpersonal relationships.

Harry's window in the same hotel as he tries to call Doris. A conflict is indicated even before Harry and Stella have established a relationship, as Harry receives a call from Miss Dolan (again fragmented in tight close-ups of her lips while she talks to him), establishing yet another triangle.

While returning from their surveillance trip, Harry and Stella find themselves on the same plane and begin to define their relationship. At first the discussion remains on a professional level, with Stella commenting that Harry gets too close to his subjects, then adding, "This is not ethical," to which Harry responds, "If we were discussing ethics, it'd be pretty silent here." Like Emily and Neil in *Remember My Name* or the inhabitants of Eve's lounge in *Choose Me,* alcohol becomes a stimulant in bringing their conversation to a more personal level. After Harry warns the stewardess that they will be ordering more drinks, they begin to discuss their private lives. When Harry indicates that he and his unnamed girlfriend are "sorta broken up now—demolished, actually," Stella begins to dispense the alleged wisdom she has presumably gained from her reading. In an echo of

Karen in *Welcome to L.A.*, she asks Harry if he is waiting for his lover and tells him, "The one who is in love always waits. . . . It's in the book." Reducing this romantic concept to a professional level again, Harry comments, "The only waiting I've been doing is outside some guy's house," and Stella responds, "Maybe you're in love with someone else."

Stella launches into a lengthy analytical dissertation about the manner in which couples crush each other under the weight of love and concludes, "So either because you want to feel guilty or because you want to show the other person how very unhappy you are, you become critical of yourself." In what could be an analysis of Coop's actions in *Trouble in Mind,* she continues, "You change your clothes, you change your habits, you change your hair. And you wait. . . . It's the lover's signature. . . . They're the ones who wait."

The more pragmatic Harry is less interested in analyzing relationships, and when Stella begins to question whether King/McGraw loves both wives, Harry asks, "Does it matter?" Nevertheless, he finds himself using some of her pop psychology observations when he meets Miss Dolan in her hotel room a short time later. As she indicates that Rick probably expects her to wait her turn, Harry tells her to give Rick up and not feel guilty or she will end up doing something like cutting her hair, adding that he likes it the way it is. While Harry is becoming more intrigued by Miss Dolan, Stella has been fired (first by Doris and then by her agency) and begins to pursue Harry. She finally corners him in his car after he has gone to talk to the neurotic Mrs. King (Annette O'Toole), and the two go to a bar, where Stella again tries to approach him on a professional level, suggesting that he needs a partner. Harry jokingly refers to her as Annie Oakley (which—given the view of the historical figure and her husband, Frank Butler, provided in Rudolph's script for *Buffalo Bill and the Indians*—does not exactly provide the best role model for a solid marital relationship), and she slaps him when he laughs at her. "That's the first time we've touched," Harry responds, once again equating romance with violence. The connection between love and pain is reinforced when Stella insists that she would have gotten more out of Mrs. King than he did, but Harry claims he did not want to hurt her. "Sometimes it helps to hurt," Stella observes.

The two decide to join forces to "save someone's life" (or, as Harry warns, to "possibly fuck it up") and seal their arrangement with a kiss, which Stella tells him comes with the slap. From this point a typically Rudolphian telepathic connection develops between them, demonstrated by Stella's ghostly presence telling Harry to call her after he breaks into Miss Dolan's hotel room (in a scene vaguely reminiscent of the detective hero's visit to the home of another ethereal heroine in the 1944 film *Laura*). The projection is reciprocated in the following scene, when Stella hears Harry's voice asking, "What if I said I'm fallin' in love with ya, Stella? What if I said that?" and Stella responds, "I'd wait for a sign, Harry." Though less audacious than the projection of Nancy into Eve's thoughts in *Choose Me*, these scenes again demonstrate Rudolph's fascination with visualizing internal desires. The incidents are all that remain of an apparent additional layer of dream imagery, described by Rudolph in an interview in *Film Comment*, which was deleted prior to the film's release. The additional material would have also emphasized the genre borrowings of the film by showing Stella's dream state as Bergmanesque images in black and white, while Harry's was made up of parodic Clint Eastwood–type scenes (Smith, 64).

The parallelism continues not just in the psychological connection between the two characters but also in their physical actions. Stella returns to McGraw's ranch and repeats Harry's earlier act of pretending to be lost and needing to use the phone. While there she witnesses a replay of the hesitant romance between McGraw's wife and the ranch hand, and she also observes a fight between McGraw and his wife. Stella makes an effort to talk to Mrs. McGraw, while Harry attempts to confront Mrs. King. Neither is initially successful, with Mrs. McGraw insisting to Stella that none of this is her business and Mrs. King accusing Harry of being the devil and claiming that nothing can threaten the love she and her husband have for each other.

After a cryptic conversation in a local bar, in which Stella tries to let McGraw know that she is aware of his double life (telling him his name fits him like a "king"), the ranch hand arrives and gets into a fight with McGraw. Stella sneaks out and returns to the ranch to convince Mrs. McGraw and her daughter to leave, only to find that she is already packed and ready to go. At the same time, Harry discovers that the man he was following is not Rick, whom he sees with Miss Dolan outside the Blue Danube. He later storms the gothic townhouse where they are staying and rescues Miss Dolan (who Rick is apparently planning to shoot) by throwing her would-be assailant out of an upper-story window. The remaining unresolved triangle comes into focus as Rudolph alternates shots of Stella arriving at the airport with shots of Harry driving Miss Dolan to the train station. Rudolph telegraphs which two sides of the triangle will end

Stella (Elizabeth Perkins, right) eavesdrops on a tryst between Mrs. McGraw (Kate Capshaw) and a ranch hand (Kevin J. O'Connor) while pretending to make a phone call. The photograph of the McGraw family on the wall next to Stella implies a normal home life, which is actually a deception.

up together by keeping Harry and Miss Dolan in separate shots during their drive, as she tells him she is feeling unloved and naked to the world (although she does not carry this to the literal extreme of Karen in *Welcome to L.A.*).

At the train station, she asks, "Is there a chance for us, Harry? For you and me?" Harry informs her that he loves someone else, and as she prepares to board the train she intimately reveals her first name and kisses him. As she boards the train she immediately encounters another man and as they disappear into the compartment Harry turns to the camera and comments, "Ah, life" (an action that is obviously intended for comic effect rather than for the introspective connotations of previous addresses to the camera in Rudolph's films).

Stella has been watching the embrace of Harry and Miss Dolan from a distance. In a gesture that recalls other Rudolph women who opt for independence rather than co-dependence, Stella dons a pair of dark glasses and leaves. In keeping with the lighter tone of the film, however, Stella does not become another of the director's unknown women (earlier she had told Harry, "You don't want to know me," and he responded, "Too late for that"). She returns to her

Miss Dolan (Anne Archer) prepares to leave Harry Dobbs (Tom Berenger) at the train station, a setting that echoes both the romantic comedies and film noirs that influenced *Love at Large*.
Courtesy Museum of Modern Art/Film Stills Archive.

apartment to find her old boyfriend (Barry Miller) waiting. As he kisses her, he tells her he wants to get back what they had before, but she slams the door on him. No sooner has she dispatched him than a pan across her apartment reveals Harry lurking behind a pillar. "What if I said I loved you?" he repeats, and Stella (who seems not at all surprised to find him there) responds, "I'd look for a sign, Harry. And not what I've been seeing lately. I'd look for some tenderness . . . sincerity." Harry promises not just a sign, but a whole billboard, as they fall onto the bed and begin to undress. Like the tentative ending of *Choose Me,* Harry questions whether their relationship will last and Stella replies that there is only one way to find out. The potential for violence surfaces one last time in a brief shot of a gun in a leg holster as Harry and Stella roll on the bed, but the film ends on a tight two-shot of them together, while Leonard Cohen returns on the soundtrack. This is shortly replaced by another musical delineation of noir romance—Warren Zevon's "Searching for a Heart" ("They say love conquers all / You can't start it like a car / You can't stop it with a gun").

   Although Rudolph regards *Love at Large* as a less personal film, he acknowledges that, like *Trouble in Mind,* it is a film made up of old movie parts: "Maybe there's a sort of benign parody involved; Tom Berenger and Elizabeth Perkins and Anne Archer . . . are taking these classic movie characters and just tweaking them" (Smith, 64). Of the three, Archer's character seems the most rooted in old movie traditions. She is in fact treated not as a character so much as a dream image that has no real existence and may be just a memory conjured up from the late show. After Harry meets her, a shot of Harry in his car dissolves into Miss Dolan singing in the nightclub, with the colors subdued, almost to the point of looking black and white, and the whole scene taking on the appearance of a dream. The camera pans to Harry sitting in the club watching her, and then an abrupt cut shows him waking up in his car. During a telephone conversation with Harry, Miss Dolan's comments become mixed with the movie being shown on the television set in his hotel room. In a later scene, they again talk on the phone, and a western is running on the television set as Miss Dolan tells Harry that Rick will kill her if he finds out she hired someone to spy on him (an action that in itself contradicts her position as one of the lovers who waits).

In contrast to Miss Dolan's otherworldly quality, Stella is more down to earth. While she is at least attempting to be a detective, she was not drawn to the profession out of a desire to live out some film-induced fantasy. Rather, she took the job in response to the deterioration of a love affair, as though searching for clues would substitute for (or perhaps enhance) the search for a perfect relationship. Like other Rudolph heroines, she not only attempts to analyze romance but also seeks assurance that her search is the right one. Karen seeks this reassurance from the camera, Eve and Pearl seek it from Dr. Love (who in turn seeks it from the morass of popular psychology she spews on the air), and Stella seeks it from *The Love Manual*. Despite her reiterated declarations from that questionable tome about the need for the one who loves to wait, Stella is aggressive in her pursuit of Harry, and her saving grace is that she does not listen to her own advice (echoing Dr. Love, who reiterates at several points in *Choose Me* that she must not take her advice too seriously). Stella's faith in romanticism is balanced by an apparent belief that she must adopt an aggressive persona to survive in a male-dominated world. Ironically, however, the more she attempts to match Harry's tough image, the more she reveals her vulnerability.

Harry seems to exist somewhere between the movie-made world of Miss Dolan and the more contemporary environment of Stella. He shares characteristics of the classic film detectives but cannot quite live up to the image. In his conversations with Miss Dolan, Harry is given some typical film noir lines that, with his gravelly delivery, end up sounding funny, whereas Miss Dolan is given the funniest lines and delivers them perfectly straight. At the same time that Harry understands Miss Dolan's special filmic language, he, like Stella, remains aware of the the problems in maintaining contemporary relationships. In Miss Dolan's world, lovers either make up, split up, or shoot each other, but in the real world relationships do not terminate so readily.

Rudolph uses Stella, Harry, and Miss Dolan to connect the viewer to the film's other characters, who represent in their own ways attributes of the three central characters. Ironically, all of these characters are so afraid of not being in love that they end up destroying the relationships they do have. Doris, who, like Stella, takes an aggressive approach to her interactions with men, allows jealousy to ruin her relationship with Harry before there is just cause for jealousy, and she inadvertantly becomes the instrument for setting up his association with Stella, who will ultimately take her place. King/McGraw is so afraid of losing love that he resorts to bigamy as a precaution, not realizing that by doing so he is in danger of losing both of the women he loves. In attempting to fulfill both relationships, he takes to extremes Stella's *Love Manual*-derived thesis about taking on new attributes to satisfy a lover: he adopts two separate personalities. It is significant that when he at last returns to Mrs. King, he drops the cowboy hat that has been identified with his other life before embracing her. Mrs. King, in turn, nearly destroys her relationship by her silence, and if she represents the one true example in the film of a lover who waits, one cannot help but feel that the reaffirmation of her faith in her lover's return comes at a price. Like Miss Dolan, Mrs. King is presented in fragmented images (shots of her hands and her knees as she fidgets nervously), suggesting that both women feel incomplete because of the tension in their relationships. This lack of a complete identity is also implied in their lack of a first name, although Miss Dolan finally tells Harry her first name at the train station when he admits he loves someone else. Unlike Mrs. King, Mrs. McGraw is in danger of destroying one relationship by her adulterous involvement in another, although it is not McGraw's discovery of her infidelity that ends their affair but his realization that by trying to maintain both marriages he is in danger of losing the one that means more to him. Of all the characters, Rudolph seems to show the least sympathy for Mrs. McGraw, who is rather conveniently sent away, with no indication that she will even renew her affair with the ranch hand. Also rather abruptly dispatched is Stella's previous boyfriend, who reappears like a deus ex machina to help her reaffirm her love for Harry. In the world that goes beyond the script, he will probably end up with Doris.

If Rudolph has had to remove much of the alternate dream world of Harry and Stella, he once again positions his characters in an environment that seems not quite real. While *Love at Large* does not place its characters in the context of a historically based myth as does *The Moderns,* it suggests a contemporary society influenced by a generation of movie-made myths. In the world these characters inhabit, urban and rural locations alike exist in a kind of haze and are generically named, with many locations in the city identified as "Metro" and those in the country bearing the name Culver (a name that provides its own old-movie associations, as though the landscapes were part of a backlot that existed at the periphery of Miss Dolan's soundstage view of the world). This generic quality even extends to slogans for local businesses: Culver Used Cars offers "The Only Deal in Town," and the Culver Café claims "The Only Meal in Town." As they pursue their desires, Rudolph's protagonists escape this generic environment into locations that evoke very specific visual images (the Blue Danube, the Sunset Motel). It is only in such places that one can imagine these characters finding their heightened romantic expectations fulfilled.

Although *Love at Large* seems to revert to the complex structure and lighter tone of *Choose Me,* it is not without connections to its immediate predecessors. The elusive Rick, like Bertram Stone in *The Moderns,* appears to regard women as objects to be possessed (although he is given little screen time and little effort is made to analyze his motives). Aspects of Stone are also apparent in King/McGraw's rather arrogant assumption that he can possess two women at the same time: like Stone, he is offered the possibility of redemption. Harry seems most allied with Hart in his tendency to objectify the objects of his desire (at least in the case of Miss Dolan). As with many of Rudolph's heroines, the women in *Love at Large* are the ones who make the greatest effort to maintain or pursue their romantic interactions. Miss Dolan, Doris, and Stella employ aggressive tactics, and even Mrs. King's willingness to wait becomes a means of maintaining her marriage, recalling Karen's initial statement in *Welcome to L.A.:* "I don't mind waiting. It's how you wait that's important anyway, I think." Harry, who does his own share of waiting (although he does not seem to know for what), takes action late in the film to sort out his desires by saving Miss Dolan from Rick and then sending her away while he returns to Stella.

Describing the film's seemingly random opening shot, Philip Strick noted in *Monthly Film Bulletin* that "all participants in *Love at Large* have something to conceal, if only from themselves, and part of the fun of the film lies in the exposure of these double lives even among the most casual bystanders."[1] While seeking to expose the literal deceptions inherent in the detective plot, the characters discover the deceptions about love, including their own. After witnessing Stella with her ex-boyfriend, Harry comments that he realized she was solving her own case, too. But, as their final questioning conversation indicates, there are some mysteries without a solution.

CHAPTER 8

Equinox: "I Have No Defense Skills!"

It is always the same: once you are liberated, you are forced to ask who you are.

—Jean Baudrillard, "Astral America" (1986)

Following the bleak vision of *Mortal Thoughts, Equinox* (1993) seeks to achieve a balance between the lighter and darker aspects of Rudolph's work. This interplay is indicated in the film's title, as well as in the opening shot of a cloudy sky that grows darker as the title appears. From this opening, the director takes us into a world of extremities, building on contrasts between poverty and power, despair and hope, reality and artificiality, destruction and redemption. As always, these themes are played out among characters who are seeking some meaning and sense of personal identity.

At the center of this study of duality are twin brothers (both played by Matthew Modine), apparently separated at birth, who inhabit the city of Empire without being aware of each other's presence. Henry has been adopted by a former-vaudevillian-turned-garage-mechanic and lives an almost hermetic existence, withdrawing from the progressively oppressive forces of the outside world. His twin, Freddy, is an assistant to the town's powerful gangster, Paris (Fred Ward), and has ambitions of achieving financial independence. For much of the film Rudolph focuses on the separate existences of the twins, while providing occasional parallels. Through them Rudolph introduces other characters, all of whom provide variations on the desire for escape. Only late in the film do the paths of the brothers converge, erupting in violence and destruction for Freddy, and forcing Henry to make the escape he has been seeking throughout the film.

Providing a framing device for the story of the twin brothers is the character of Sonya (Tyra Ferrell), a morgue attendent who is writing a short story during breaks from her job. When the body of a woman who died on the street is brought in, Sonya impulsively steals a letter from her belongings and discovers that it reveals a fairy-tale-like account of the twins, who were born to a ballerina after she had an affair with a married count. These details are revealed slowly during the course of the film and presented in highly stylized, artificially lighted scenes. Although Sonya remains on the periphery throughout most of the film, she becomes the means through which the complete story is revealed (but not, ironically, to the two main characters). Like Rudolph's other poets, she becomes involved in the events but also comments on them from the position of an outsider, and the establishment of her story-writing at the outset suggests that what follows may in fact be only her creation.

The concept of duality is established in the opening scenes. In a sequence recalling Wim Wenders's 1988 film *Wings of Desire* (also about the potential for redemption in an oppressive environment), the camera dissolves from the dark sky to ominous images of skyscrapers, and then cranes down past the American flags hanging from the buildings to the homeless people huddled on the street outside the Empire federal building. The polarized concepts of light and dark are matched by the impression of great power and abject poverty. Even the redemption motif is ironically contradicted in this opening, as an apparently homeless woman is seen trying to help a dying companion while telling her, "I ain't no angel." The dying woman is Helena, who has the letter that Sonya will soon find.

In addition to establishing extremities, this opening scene emphasizes the city itself as a force in encouraging the false hopes of its inhabitants. Unlike *Trouble in Mind*'s Rain City (which implies a mood) or *Love at Large*'s Metro (which suggests a contrast to the film's rural settings), the name Empire indicates concepts of money and power (Rudolph shot the film, appropriately, in the Twin Cities, although this is a rather elaborate inside joke, as he has made the Minnesota locations largely unrecognizable). Rather than encouraging spiritual and moral development, the city seems resigned to its own corruption. A constant presence in the film are signs and announcements for Lotto, which offer the dream of financial stability as the ultimate goal. The seductive power of wealth is made even more obvious in later shots of Paris (his name alone carrying an urban association) watching stock market reports, which are presented on television under footage of nude women. Like Stone in *The Moderns,* Paris's financial power becomes equated with objectification and a kind of dehumanization of sexuality. Even basic survival is merchandised, as demonstrated by the television commercials that offer self-defense training (the woman being assaulted in the commercial turns to the camera and cries, "I have no defense skills!"). Rudolph has said of the film's environment, "The lottery to me seems to be the summary of the Big Lies that we're told. The thing is, life is like the lottery, only in life you have half a chance of winning. . . . And there's always the workers digging up the streets, making noise and basically never improving anything, in an industrial society that's not producing anything, it's just sort of going nowhere" (Smith, 63).

While the lottery may represent the Big Lie, money becomes a motivating factor for many of the characters in *Equinox.* In addition to the gangsters, money influences peripheral characters, such as Henry's mechanic father who hopes to sell his garage to a developer so his son can visit the places he dreams about. More self-centered is Sonya, the apparent conjurer of the events, who tells a co-worker at the outset that she is hoping the story she writes will "raise me out of the junk." She later discovers that she is entitled to a share of the trust fund left for the two brothers and becomes visibly excited when told that it amounts to several million dollars. Ironically, Freddy's wife (Lori Singer) frantically scratches away at mountains of lottery tickets in an attempt to win a better life; neither she nor Freddy is aware that he is heir to a fortune.

Those characters who have not been able to work within the city's power structure have found solace in dreams of escape, or have retreated into a fantasy life, which constitutes its own form of escape. After fighting off the thugs on the street who try to steal his few meager purchases, Henry locks himself (with multiple locks) in an apartment whose walls are covered with posters for places he longs to visit. His friend Russell (Kevin J. O'Connor) continually urges him to renew a relationship with Russell's sister Beverly (Lara Flynn Boyle), but Henry keeps resisting his invitations to meet for dinner. Secretly Henry calls Beverly, and each time she answers the phone he freezes and is unable to speak. Beverly, in turn, isolates herself in her apartment, where she dances alone, reads Emily Dickinson (a fitting choice for Beverly's secluded existence), and has taken to talking about herself in the third person. While trying to encourage their relationship, Russell is reluctant to act on his own desire for Anna (Angel Aviles), a waitress at the restaurant where the lives of the twin brothers will ultimately intersect.

Henry is also hesitant about interfering in the life of his next door neighbor Rosie (Marisa Tomei), a prostitute regularly abused by her pimp (who sports a Roy Orbison look). Rosie eventually forces herself into Henry's life, showing up at his door to dump her baby off on him while she goes to work, and later returning to "thank him properly." Rosie, like *Made in Heaven*'s Lucille, provides a source of temptation that sidetracks the hero from his goals, although her baby also provides a connection to the angelic Georgia of *Trouble in Mind*. Her role as temptress is indicated when she comes to Henry's apartment to repay him for caring for her baby. As she enters the apartment, the camera does a rack focus to an apple sitting on a table in the foreground with a knife through it, an image rife with biblical connotations. When she begins to go down on Henry, he covers his face with a pillow, and the camera cuts to Beverly dancing alone in her apartment with a pillow (appropriately, to the song "Temptation"), establishing a connection between them while reinforcing Beverly as a symbol of innocence from which Henry is being seduced away.

After their encounter, Rosie disillusions Henry by referring to the "job" she just did. She also expresses her desire to attain the good life like everyone else, and as she talks she and Henry are framed in a two-shot, with another Lotto billboard visible through the window between them. While Rosie does not seek to escape from the city itself, she has her own goals, which consist of getting off the streets and moving inside with her escorts, "just like *Pretty Women* [sic]." Ultimately, like the other characters who seek goals within the city's power structure rather than in opposition to it, Rosie pays for her dreams with her life.

This concept is reinforced in the destructive path of Freddy and his hot-headed partner, Richie (Tate Donovan), a relationship that parallels and contrasts the association of Henry and Russell. Richie has ambitions of moving up in the organization and becoming driver to Paris, although his aspirations will be ended by a bullet through his skull in a dark alley, courtesy of Freddy. Freddy's own demise takes longer, and his ambitions are much greater. Recalling Coop in *Trouble in Mind*, he indicates to his wife (who continually tells him, "You're the best") that the best thing for them to do would be to make a lot of money and then get the hell out of town.

Freddy's downfall proves to be not ambition but ambiguity. His wife comments that he grew up with no family and no memories, and she takes credit for redeeming him. Reinforcing the twins motif, Freddy replies, "Before I met you I was just half a man, but now everything has changed." He echoes this self-assurance later when Paris observes that it must be weird for Freddy not knowing who he is supposed to grow up to be like, and Freddy responds, "There's certain advantages. . . . You grow up to be yourself." As the film progresses, however, there is evidence that this professed independence masks a sense of self-doubt, and Freddy seems to be seeking to define himself. To demonstrate Freddy's internal search, Rudolph relies on familiar devices, with Freddy continually studying his appearance in mirrors or looking, if not directly into the camera, then at least away from other characters in a shot.

Freddy's search for identity is paralleled by Henry's sense of displacement. When he finally agrees to meet Beverly for dinner, she tells him, "You have to face yourself, Henry. You have to face the real you. We all have a real you. Not your you, but our own." Henry responds, "My whole life seems to be taking place without me in it," and Beverly replies, "Maybe you're schizophrenic . . . you know, split

Director Rudolph (left) consults with Matthew Modine on the set of *Equinox* (1993). Although in this scene Modine is playing Freddy Ace, the more violent of the two twins, his position at the piano suggests his potential for artistic expression.

personality." Long before they meet, the two brothers begin experiencing aspects of each other's personalities, with Freddy becoming more uncertain, while Henry begins to act more aggressively. Henry even takes on Rosie's pimp and throws him down a flight of stairs (in a fantasy moment, Rudolph cuts in a shot of Henry made up like the hero of telelvision self-defense commercials). That neither brother is completely good or evil is indicated when Freddy's wife tells him, "You're not nearly as wicked as people say," at about the same time that Henry is becoming more forceful in his pursuit of Beverly (presumably brought on by his sexual encounter with Rosie). Late in the film Henry tells Russell that he loves Beverly and adds, "Maybe I'm finally facing myself like she said." What he finds when he faces himself is still not complete, however, and he observes, "I was sure that one day something was gonna jump out at me. That either it would be another bad sign and destroy me right there, or it would help me to figure out the whole damn mess."

As Henry is saying this, Freddy and an associate are shown driving up to the restaurant where Henry and Russell are meeting. While Henry's search for meaning is just beginning, Freddy implies to Anna that his has ended; he tells her, "It doesn't mean anything. Not any of it does. It's like nature. The leaf drinks the water. The bug eats the leaf. The frog eats the bug, croaks and then dies in the water. One big circle. It doesn't mean a goddamn thing." Having made this existential observation, Freddy descends into chaos. A fight breaks out in the restaurant, and Russell is knocked out by Freddy's associate, Dandridge (Gailard Sartain), who then fights with Henry (echoing an earlier altercation between Henry and Rosie's pimp and indicating that Henry, like Russell, is forced to resort to violence in his efforts to help others). After Anna shoots Dandridge, Freddy finds himself face to face with his twin and the moment is suspended in time, with events unfolding in slow motion as Freddy is shot and Henry responds as though he has been hit. Freddy stumbles out, and Henry follows the trail of blood to an alley. For the first time the brothers are shown in the same shot, as Freddy dies in front of a Lotto sign.

The confrontation of the two brothers provides the sign of which Henry had earlier spoken to Russell. Rather than helping him to "figure out the whole damn mess," however, it leaves him more uncertain. Nevertheless, it motivates his escape. He stops long enough to try to convince Beverly to leave with him, but she does not understand and ends up remaining in her apartment building, the Sheltering Arms, while Henry drives off. Later Sonya arrives to try to explain things to her. Like Karen reverting back to her repeated phrases while talking to Linda at the end of *Welcome to L.A.,* Beverly returns to referring to herself in the third person as the two women talk.

It is Sonya who sums up the dominant motif of the film when she tells Beverly, "The way I figure it, your whole life is about searching for one thing. And all that other stuff just falls away." As she says this, Henry is shown driving on the open road. During a stop at the Monument Diner, Henry sees a woman with twin boys and, after running out, sees his multiple reflection in the mirrored glass of a phone booth. In the film's breathtaking ending, Henry finds himself standing at the edge of the Grand Canyon (which he had earlier told Beverly he wanted to visit "before they tear it down"), and the camera circles him several times as he stares into the abyss; finally it tightens in on him, and whispered voices are heard. These whispers are heard again over shots of the story being written during the final credits, reinforcing the notion that all that has been seen has been created, or perhaps suggesting that a new story is starting to be written. This bravura finale may seem to leave Henry lost and literally on the edge, but it also has a redemptive quality. Henry's epiphany has left him poised on the precipice of a great discovery and, in the process of finding out that everything he has believed up to this point to be true is not, he at last is forced to face up to himself and the meaning of his life. The image of the story being written as the final credits roll—the implication of a "creator"—carries a spiritual connotation that, like the resurrection of Stone in *The Moderns,* offers hope for an escape from the materialism of modern society. With regard to the ambiguity of the finale, Rudolph has said,

> It doesn't mean anything and yet it seems fraught with meaning—it's basically an interpretive ending. People said it would have been better if he'd called her and they had talked and I said, "Well, that costs a quarter." If the blanks were filled in for him, he'd still be as crippled as he was at the beginning. But the fact that this guy has the illusion of knowing that his life might have been different than he was led to believe, suddenly has found a meaning inside of himself—the movie ends at a beginning basically—so then he might be able to fill in almost every blank and have the strength to accept it. (Smith, 64)

The circular camerawork at the Grand Canyon reinforces the fact that Henry's quest has come full circle, back to a point in childhood when he knew the truth but did not yet have the capacity to retain it. Aside from the impressive ending shot, Rudolph uses conscious stylistic devices throughout the film to defy perceptions of reality. The flashback scenes are presented in a dominant yellow (almost sepia-toned) tint, implying a nostalgic glow but also indicating that what is being shown may not be literal. The aura of unreality is reinforced in the appearance of an obviously artificial painted ship at the dock, much like the one on which Hart and Oiseau sail for America in *The Moderns*.

Despite the unreal quality of the flashbacks, elements from the past carry over to the present. The art deco look of some of these scenes is echoed in the painting *Stolen Moments* that Freddy's wife has purchased in redecorating their apartment. While the Count represents wealth and power, Helena is identified as a dancer, and her artistic nature is reinforced in the statues and paintings of ballerinas Beverly has in her apartment. That the whole story may be another of Sonya's creations is suggested by the fact that on the wall of the diner where Sonya writes her story is a program for the Empire Orchestra that contains a photograph of a ballerina. Significantly, in the diner where Henry sees the mother with twin boys at the end of the film, a display rack contains postcards with pictures of dancers—a seemingly incongruous image for this desert café but one that provides another piece to the puzzle Henry is struggling to solve.

Beverly (Lara Flynn Boyle) emulates the dancer in a painting while in the solitude of her apartment.

The dreamlike qualities that dominate the flashbacks only occasionally surface in the present and, as in other Rudolph films, imply a telepathic connection between characters. During Beverly and Henry's meeting at the restaurant, the camera pans between them as they begin a private conversation. Rudolph isolates them in individual close-ups as Beverly talks about the last time they saw each other; but Henry suddenly appears on the opposite side of Beverly, caressing her cheek with his lips as she talks, an image expressing her private desires. The image might also be taken as related to the doubling concept that is crucial to the film, particularly as Beverly will tell Henry a short time later that he might be a split personality. Later, when they return to her apartment Henry begins to get passionate, but Beverly tells him she does not want him to be more aggressive. In a disorienting shot, Henry appears to leave her apartment, then returns from the other side of the screen to kiss her. The most audacious defiance of our perceptions of reality is reserved for Beverly at the end of the film. As Henry is looking at his reflection in the door of the phone booth outside the diner, there is a cut to Beverly alone in her apartment standing in a mirror image of the pose of a dancer in a painting on the wall. The camera moves in to her hand as she reaches for the phone, and when it returns to her face the painting behind her has been replaced by a poster of palm trees like the ones in Henry's apartment. This shot suggests her connection to Henry, but it also might suggest her withdrawal into a more private form of escape.

Rudolph also uses dream imagery to indicate memories. After Rosie is killed, Henry returns to his apartment, and Rudolph repeats a shot of her standing in front of a poster of a castle. As Henry yanks the poster from the wall and crumples it up, Beverly is heard in voice-over reading from Emily Dickinson's poem "I Cannot Meet the Spring Unmoved." Another memory shot is presented after Freddy's death, when he suddenly appears in his apartment as his wife awakens from a nightmare.

As always, a significant element in creating the dreamlike atmosphere is Rudolph's use of music. The director commented that Mark Isham was unavailable and the budget did not allow for a composer, so he picked out prerecorded music that he thought would not be costly (Smith, 67). These limitations actually freed him to select a wide range of music that provided distinct motifs for each character. Jazz is used for scenes between Freddy and his wife; comic Broadway-type scoring is used to introduce scenes at the garage where

Henry and his adopted father easily slip into vaudeville bits while working; and Muzak versions of romantic songs are associated with Beverly (the aforementioned "Temptation" and the even more appropriate "I'm in the Mood for Love"). Perhaps the most striking musical motif is the chanting that accompanies shots of Sonya pursuing the story of the twins. The music adds a dynamic quality to her scenes, particularly a tracking shot down rows of bookshelves while she is conducting research. More important, this cue provides the final clue that what we have witnessed may be Sonya's creation, as it appears again during the final credits over the shots of the story being written.

The notion that Sonya is creating what we see adds a fairy-tale dimension to the film, which takes some of the edge off its bleak vision. Rudolph has said that he considered using the phrase "Once upon a Time" at the outset to reinforce this concept. He also acknowledges, however, that the original script was much grittier and more realistic, but he modified it after he made *Mortal Thoughts* (Smith, 60). The film was originally titled *In the Blood,* a phrase that echoes a familiar Rudolph refrain heard in Baskin's lyrics for *Welcome to L.A.* and in the dialogue for *Choose Me.* In addition to its connotations of both passion and violence, the references that remain in *Equinox* to "blood things" equate the concept to familial relationships and the feeling that people are connected. This provides a degree of hope in a film that the director admits is about "people who are isolated and not trying terribly hard to connect, or are very, very poor at it" (Smith, 63). He also observes, "I'd simply held up a mirror on society. This is as close as I've come to doing that. Even though it's fictional, it's the same as all the films I write and direct: people trying to connect in a crazy world. But this film is also about an uncaring society, about people lying to themselves, about people whose fantasy lives become as important as their real, daily lives."[1] In his next film, *Mrs. Parker and the Vicious Circle,* Rudolph would use a nonfictional subject to examine people whose fantasy lives became inseparable from their real lives and who found themselves connected and isolated at the same time.

CHAPTER 9

Director for Hire: The Relationship between Styrofoam and the Planet Jupiter

Hollywood likes my eye, they just don't like what I see. What Hollywood does to its most talented offspring is pay them a lot of money to behave like artists as long as they don't produce any art.

—Alan Rudolph, *Artforum* (January 1993)

As I indicated in the Preface, Rudolph's career has been divided between projects he created and those for which he was brought on as director. Rudolph regards his "director-for-hire" films as less personal than his other work, but in many ways they provide a clearer indication of his view of contemporary American society. Many of his personal films take place in a world that looks familiar but has an air of unreality, and although they are shot on recognizable locations, Rudolph refashions the settings to conform to his personal vision. Even when a scene in *Trouble in Mind,* for example, is obviously filmed in the Space Needle in Seattle, the location blends into the texture of Rudolph's futuristic Rain City. But productions such as *Roadie* (1980), *Endangered Species* (1982), *Songwriter* (1985), and *Mortal Thoughts* (1991) take place in defined settings that cover a cross-section of American society. The documentary *Return Engagement* provides obvious comment on the two decades that preceded its 1983 release through the use of two cultural icons, Timothy Leary and G. Gordon Liddy. Even the more fanciful *Made in Heaven* (1987) reflects on the moral ambiguity and aimlessness of contemporary American society.

Although different in tone, *Roadie, Endangered Species,* and *Songwriter* involve a quest that requires the protagonist to leave his own environment, as opposed to the characters of Carroll in *Welcome to L.A.* and Emily in *Remember My Name,* both of whom have to return to the landscape of their past and confront it before they can move on. In *Roadie* and *Endangered Species* this quest takes the form of a literal trek. In the former, Travis W. Redfish (Meat Loaf) makes this journey to win Lola Bouilliabase (Kaki Hunter), while in *Endangered Species* Ruben Castle (Robert Urich) leaves New York for Colorado, ostensibly on a vacation, but in doing so recovers the connection to family he had lost in the city. Like Ruben, Doc Jenkins (Willie Nelson) in *Songwriter* seeks to reinstate the family bond he has severed, although his journey, like that of Carroll and Emily, is not a literal outward trek as much as an internal search backward into his own past. *Made in Heaven* combines the two forms of journeys by having protagonist Mike/Elmo confront his past in the course of a quest to find his identity and the bonds he formed in heaven. The films are also united by the presentation of independent protagonists who find themselves at odds with an established social system, whether it is the music business in *Roadie* and *Songwriter,* the government in *Endangered Species,* or even the afterlife in *Made in Heaven.* This spirit of individualism extends to the protagonists of *Return Engagement.* Demonstrating the director's individualistic spirit by signaling his return to independent filmmaking, this film provides the most direct summation of Rudolph's attitude toward success and the manufacturing of images in American society. The documentary format carries an inherent orientation toward the search for truth, and Rudolph provides a more dramatic analysis of the concept in *Mortal Thoughts.* In his director-for-hire films Rudolph depicts an America that has become commercialized, profit-oriented, paranoid, fatalistic, and able to package its crimes as entertainment, but where salvation can be achieved through basic human interaction and independence can still win out over oppressive social systems. These themes have carried through in his more personal work, although the vision in his later films has become even darker and the obstacles that his idealistic heroes have to overcome far more dangerous.

SKELETONS IN THE DESERT,
SKELETONS IN THE CLOSET

Prior to *Welcome to L.A.* Rudolph received directing credit for two low-budget horror films made around the time he began his apprenticeship with Altman. Given Rudolph's own expressed indifference to these films, it is more appropriate to consider them in terms of Rudolph's less personal projects. Yet, if the films offer little or no evidence of an emerging directorial style, they do occasionally offer intriguing connections to Rudolph's later work.

Premonition (1970), in particular, shows early indications of some of the director's chief concerns. Produced by Rudolph's father, the film concerns a student, Neil (Carl Crow), who accompanies a professor into the desert in search of a lost Indian tribe. They discover an Indian skeleton with a mummified face, as well as a mysterious plant with red flowers that the professor claims caused the Indians to hallucinate themselves to death when smoked. Their truck crashes while transporting the skeleton, and the experience has a disturbing effect on Neil. As he and two friends form a band and try to get auditions, Neil begins having hallucinations about a mysterious shadowy figure. While rehearsing in a farmhouse near San Francisco, Neil and fellow musician Andy (Tim Ray) share a dream in which Andy is attacked by the figure. Following an unsuccessful audition, the group throws a party at the farmhouse and Andy wanders off. Neil again envisions the assault and Andy is later found dead from a head wound. In an *Invasion of the Body Snatchers*–like finale, a car is shown transporting the mysterious red flowers.

Besides its science fiction resonance, the film owes much to the drug culture of the late 1960s, with its continual references to marijuana and other stimulants. Shots of Andy and associate Baker (Winfrey Hester Hill) riding motorcycles along the shoreline owe an obvious debt to *Easy Rider* (1969), an open-air audition is presented as a small-scale *Woodstock* (1970), and even Andy's appearance seems to be modeled after Arlo Guthrie in *Alice's Restaurant* (1969). Yet, along with its obvious borrowings, the film offers foreshadowing of Rudolph's later work. This is particularly apparent in the concept of the inability to distinguish between reality and a dream state, and in the telepathic bond that develops between Neil and Andy, which anticipates the psychic bond that will link later Rudolph characters, such as Nancy and Eve in *Choose Me*. The dream sequences provide the first evidence of Rudolph's structural experiments with viewpoint, as they represent a shared vision that cannot be attributed exclusively to one character. Counteracting this is a more direct acknowledgment of viewpoint in Neil's address to the camera—a device Rudolph will again incorporate in *Welcome to L.A.*

Premonition also offers, however briefly, one of the first of Rudolph's triangular relationships, and one that involves a nonhuman element. At one point Andy's decision to form a band with Neil causes him to leave his girlfriend, with whom he allegedly has an open relationship. While it might be argued that Neil forms the third side of the triangle and the destructive force in ending their association, he is actually representative of Andy's commitment to an artistic pursuit—specifically music—that undoubtedly would have caused a rift in the relationship even without Neil as catalyst. One of the director's favorite stylistic devices, consisting of a move from a two-shot into a close-up that serves to isolate one of the characters, is effectively employed in the scene in which Neil convinces Andy to come with him to form a band and the camera zooms in to isolate Andy's girlfriend, whom he will soon leave behind.

In addition to its structural aspects, the film contains individual elements that anticipate later films. Another example of isolation—a shot of Andy alone on a rock on the shoreline—anticipates the more dramatic final image of Matthew Modine at the rim of the Grand Canyon in *Equinox*. A negative attitude toward financial success is expressed in references to Andy's family having made a fortune in the plumbing business, which he rejects (although Andy's parents are unseen, the implied relationship is a warm-up for the father-son relationship of Carl and Carroll in *Welcome to L.A.*). There is even a hint of social commentary in the prejudicial attitudes of the townspeople toward black musician Baker.

Aside from such references (which are only of interest in hindsight) and a few stylistic innovations (such as a tracking shot of Andy in the woods which creates a feeling of floating), there is little to recommend the film. Writing about the movie years later when it was released on video (as *The Impure*), Philip Strick commented in *Monthly Film Bulletin*, "Looking tolerantly at the film's ventures into uneasy relationships, some predecessors might be discerned for Rudolph's subsequent gallery of probationers, carrying the imprisoned past in their wild eyes and their erratic assaults on normality. As well as protesting the degenerative legacy of a dope-addicted decade, *Premonition* could be seen as a first sketch for *Trouble in Mind*, its gaunt storyteller as much of a ruin as El

Gavillan [Hawk], and both of them finishing up on an endless highway."[1]

Much less defensible is Rudolph's second directorial credit, *Terror Circus* (also titled *Barn of the Naked Dead* and released on video as *Nightmare Circus*). Those critics who have complained of sexist attitudes in *Welcome to L.A.* and other films would find great support for their argument in this reprehensible account of a psychopath (Andrew Prine) who keeps women chained in a barn and forces them, with the aid of a bullwhip, to perform for him like circus animals. The connections to Rudolph's later work are even more tenuous than in *Premonition*. One would have to stretch a point to regard the scene in which a nightclub owner argues with the manager of three female performers who have disappeared as a reflection on financial control of artists. There are also references to unnatural child-parent relationships in the psychopath's attraction to a woman he believes is his missing mother and in the discovery that his father has become a hideous mutant as a result of radiation experiments in the area, but these owe more to the perverse parental relationships of post-*Psycho* slasher flicks than to any of Rudolph's other work.

Mainly, the film is a series of scenes depicting the torture of women, which Rudolph presents with some obvious directorial choices, such as shooting through bars to create the feeling of cages (a device he will employ to greater effect in *Remember My Name*). Rudolph's sympathies at least appear to be with the victims rather than their torturer and he devotes more screen time to their attempts at escape than to the brutalities to which they are subjected; but this is scant compensation for scenes such as a woman being smeared with blood and then stalked by a carnivorous animal or another being bound and having a snake crawl between her legs. In his defense, Rudolph claims to have been brought onto the project after filming began and was not involved in its creation. He states that he worked on the film for five or six days and never saw the final cut. Rudolph seems understandably reluctant to discuss these early skeletons in his cinematic closet, and they are best viewed today, if at all, as mere footnotes to his filmography rather than as indicators of the emergence of a major cinematic talent.

ROADIE

When funding for *The Moderns* fell through after the poor distribution of *Welcome to L.A.* and *Remember My Name*, Rudolph had diffi-

culty finding work. He accepted an assignment from Carolyn Pfeiffer
to direct *Roadie* and, following the luxury of working at Lion's Gate
with Robert Altman, found himself working within a studio system.
Rudolph has stated that *Roadie* "is what it is: a comic book"
(Rudolph 1985, 264). It is certainly hard to imagine a more drastic
change of pace from the dark brooding atmosphere of *Remember My
Name*. Although critics regarded *Welcome to L.A.* as demonstrating
the influence of Altman, *Roadie* is in many ways closer to the expansive, freewheeling style of Altman's early work, and its exaggerated
characters, particularly the outlandish Redfish family, actually seem
closest in spirit to the later (1987) film *O. C. and Stiggs*. (The same
year *Roadie* was released Altman directed his own live-action cartoon, *Popeye*).

The great irony here—and it is an entertaining one—is that the
"ordinary" characters in Rudolph's film are much more bizarre than

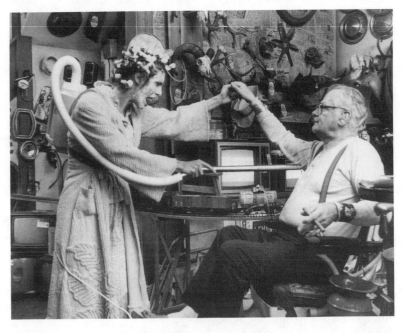

In *Roadie* (1980), Alice Poo Redfish (Rhonda Bates) vacuums her father,
Corpus (Art Carney), in the cluttered confines of the Redfish domicile.
Rudolph attempts to create a live-action cartoon set in a world in which
everything is salvageable.
Courtesy Museum of Modern Art/Film Stills Archive.

the rock stars in the film, at least when the music performers are off-stage. Debbie Harry and Roy Orbison are quite down to earth when encountered in honkytonk bars, and even the outrageous Alice Cooper is thoroughly average when seen without makeup, costume, and snake. The film continues Rudolph's interest, first demonstrated in *Buffalo Bill,* with the conflict between actual and manufactured images, but in this case the audience is aware of these images and a conspirator in their creation.

While the locations of *Roadie* are specific places—from Austin, Texas, to Los Angeles to New York—Rudolph offers his own warped, off-kilter view of an America in which everything is salvageable, everyone is identified by description rather than name and knowledge is acquired by reading T-shirts. Moving through it all is the optimistic spirit of Travis W. Redfish (Meat Loaf), whose motto—"Everything will work out if you let it"—is established in the opening song. To indicate his symbolic nature, Rudolph first presents the formidable salvage man (in a shot that is also a parody of the "star" entrances of old Hollywood) as he descends from the heavens in front of an American flag, and the film becomes an affirmation, after a decade plagued by national crises, that society as a whole is salvageable.

Travis is portrayed as an innocent who has never left the state of Texas. That changes, however, when he spots Lola, "the first woman I ever cared for as a human being." Although she fancies herself a groupie, Lola (Kaki Hunter), too, is one of life's innocents (she later tells Travis she is a virgin, but only because she is saving herself for Alice Cooper). She and Travis anticipate other innocents in Rudolph's films, such as Georgia in *Trouble in Mind* and Henry in *Equinox,* who somehow manage to survive the corruption around them. Whether dealing with drug dealers or shady promoters, Travis and Lola are able to maintain their basic integrity and honesty.

If Travis views the universe as an accident waiting for repair, Lola sees it as a giant cosmic force, generated by the manufactured images she so admires. During their initial encounter she tells Travis, "Rock and roll is the greatest energy of our time and groupies are the spark plugs of rock and roll," to which the less metaphysical Travis responds, "Oh, yeah. . . . I'm sort of a fuel pump myself." The disparity between her ethereal and his practical visions is made more pronounced in a later scene in which she again reasserts her belief that rock and roll is the greatest energy, and Travis counters that the greatest energy is manure. He proceeds to prove his point by using dung to fuel the equipment for a concert after it has been shut down for wasting energy. Lola also claims a psychic gift, but only when it comes to "rock and roll and the cosmic mechanism" and other "stuff" she really cares about. By contrast, Travis has a tendency, when hit, to go into "brainlock" and contemplate such imponderables as "What's the relationship between Styrofoam and the planet Jupiter?"

Lola strives to conform to her notion of how a groupie should appear and to adopt the look of the performers she admires (she even applies Alice Cooper–style makeup after meeting the rock star), whereas Travis attempts to maintain his individuality in a world in which people are reduced to descriptions that draw on comparisons to other show business types. Concert promoter Don Cornelius is described as "the ringmaster of the rock and roll circus," and he, in turn, refers to Travis as "the Ali of roadies." Even Travis adopts the language when he tells Lola he read an article that described Alice Cooper as "the Bela Lugosi of rock and roll." Travis's assertion of individuality culminates in his refusal to go on the road with Cooper's band because his sister is getting married and he considers that more important, even if it means sacrificing Lola. In the end, she gives up her show business fantasies in favor of life on the road with Travis and discovers, in the final shot, that there are stranger things in the universe than were dreamt of in her rock and roll philosophy.

The reduction of human beings to tag lines is appropriate to a world dominated by pop-culture images. Rudolph's later film *The Moderns* depicts an environment in which art is being taken over by commercialization and advertising. *Roadie,* in its good-natured way, indicates that the concept has been taken to a degree where human beings have become walking advertisements and emotions are packaged. Even Travis's heartfelt attempt to reconcile with Lola at one point is transmogrified into entertainment. As a band performs onstage, Travis and Lola argue back and forth into microphones, and their discourse becomes an instant new-wave song in a case of life imitating art rock.

Television becomes an omnipresent force and is constantly on view, even when events in the real world are more exciting. During a chase through the streets of Austin, the television in Cornelius's limo is showing "The Hank and Jerry Show," a static talking-head discussion. As Rudolph presents a deep focus shot down a main street while the participants in the chase zigzag back and forth on the cross streets, one of the TV show's hosts comments that when the filmmaker Mack Sennett did chase scenes people were actually killed, and his colleague laments that nobody dies for comedy anymore. A connection between television and the real world is also indicated in a later scene in a hotel room, as Travis watches *The Incredible Shrinking Man* (which he thinks is a *National Geographic* special) while Lola is fighting off "a spider the size of an armadillo"). In the end, as Travis rides off to find Lola, his father turns off the bank of television sets in Redfish Manor (itself a veritable museum of disposable popular culture), suggesting a potential victory for reality. The final shot of Travis and Lola encountering a UFO indicates, however, that they cannot escape the realm of the fantastic and that the real world will prove far more bizarre than the one we have manufactured for our entertainment. It is a theme that would carry over into Rudolph's next film, *Endangered Species*.

In what might be a parody of Brian De Palma's *Carrie* (1976), a beauty queen becomes the unfortunate victim of a confrontation between Lola Bouilli-abase (Kaki Hunter) and Travis W. Redfish (Meat Loaf).
Courtesy Museum of Modern Art/Film Stills Archive.

Typically, *Roadie* generated mixed responses, with some critics appreciating its amiable spirit and energy, while others objected that the production was unfocused and incoherent. The film appears to be an amalgam of comedy techniques. The numerous bar fights and chase scenes try for a slapstick quality, while at other points Rudolph indulges in comic wordplay. The verbal humor is most apparent in a conversation in a laundromat in which federal agents try to confront Travis and Lola about drug dealers while they are arguing about their relationship, leading to an increasingly absurdist exchange. After the controlled elegance of *Remember My Name, Roadie* seems to be a film in search of a style and seems something of an oddity, not only in relation to the films that preceded it but also to the one to follow.

ENDANGERED SPECIES

The UFO image that ended *Roadie* provides the starting point for *Endangered Species,* although the tone of the film is significantly different from its predecessor. This time, the explanation for the strange lights in the sky is less fantastic but far more dangerous. Derived from actual events, *Endangered Species* most closely conforms to the political paranoia thrillers common in the 1970s (many of which were produced even before the actual events of Watergate made the concept of a government conspiracy no longer the stuff of speculation). Yet, in presenting this account of secret germ warfare tests being performed on cattle, Rudolph also focuses on the issue of dehumanization and the impact of advanced technology on society. Ultimately, the film calls for some reclamation of human values through its depiction of the reestablishment of a family unit.

The concept of dehumanization is established in an early shot in which Rudolph dissolves from a cattle stampede to a city street crowded with faceless masses. The sense of anonymity is reinforced as the camera tracks toward one of a series of indistinguishable windows in a skyscraper. Inside an office, the cop Ruben (Robert Urich) is being interviewed. Paralleling the human-cattle connection, he refers to his body as a "carcass." Ruben establishes the theme of opposition to a corrupt system when he complains that he spends his time catching criminals, only to have the judges let them out of prison after he gets them convicted.

These early scenes indicate a conflict between authority and family, with Ruben's work as a cop having caused a rift between him and his teenage daughter. He tries to reconcile with her by telling her he has sobered up and quit his job. Ruben hopes to reestablish their relationship by taking a vacation in Colorado. Once there, the conflict between authority and family surfaces again, as he becomes caught up in investigating mysterious cattle mutilations, and the theme is reinforced in the presence of policewoman Harriet Purdue (JoBeth Williams). The two characters are connected through their professions as well as through references to their drinking problems and the fact that both were in the army. Rudolph reinforces the parallels visually in a cut from Ruben alone in his trailer to Harriet working alone in her office. Harriet's position as authoritarian seems to have led to a suppression of her feminine side (she even goes by the name Harry rather than Harriet, and a cattleman's assistant calls her "sir"), although she objects to Ruben's masculine aggressiveness.

The importance of the family unit is most pronounced in a scene in which Ruben goes to visit friend Joe Hiatt (Paul Dooley), who runs the local newspaper. Rudolph provides a three-shot, with

Cops Harriet Purdue (JoBeth Williams) and Ruben Castle (Robert Urich) must join forces to solve a series of cattle mutilations in *Endangered Species* (1982). This publicity still suggests the atmosphere of paranoia that pervades the film.
Courtesy Museum of Modern Art/Film Stills Archive.

Ruben framed by Joe and his wife, and then zooms in to isolate Ruben in close-up, indicating his separation from a traditional family structure. The notion of separation within a potential family unit is further demonstrated in a deep-focus shot after Joe's death, with Harriet inside a house, in the foreground on the phone, Ruben's daughter standing alone outside the house and Ruben in the background getting into a car—the three of them in the same shot but isolated. Even when Ruben decides to send his daughter away for her protection, Rudolph films their embrace before she boards a plane in individual close-ups so that the two of them are not shown together in a single shot. The daughter is kidnapped before she can escape, and it is only when Ruben and Harriet join forces to rescue her that the conspiracy is also exposed, suggesting that it is family as much as authority that is necessary for survival.

Unlike many conspiracy films, the opposing force in this film is not the government itself, but rather a group of ultrapatriotic soldiers of fortune whose experiments with germ warfare are being conducted with the intention of eventually using the results on the Soviets. The experiments are being supported by local cattlemen, and a dichotomy is established between capitalism/militarism and the individualism/ idealism reflected by Joe. The newspaper editor is killed when he tries to find out about the conspiracy, and cattleman Ben Morgan (Hoyt Axton) is also dispatched (in a particularly grisly scene) when he decides the plot has gone too far. Throughout the development of the conspiracy, the affiliation and political orientation of the conspirators is not defined, and, as Ruben points out, it does not really matter if it is the far Left or the far Right if one gets in their way.

This sense of an anonymous but powerful force that randomly assigns death is both a reflection of and a contributor to the dehumanization of society. At one point the mercenary behind the experiments informs Ben that a number of people are starting to look like cows to him. The paranoia created by a climate in which anyone can become a potential target is expressed by Ruben when he claims there are bad guys everywhere. Although Harriet dismisses the comment by responding that his years on the streets have made him paranoid, she later realizes the truth of his assertion. This paranoia leads to a feeling of entrapment, which is once again reinforced through Rudolph's familiar device of shooting characters through bars, glass partitions, and other barriers.

Even though opening and ending statements attempt to ground the film in actual events, Rudolph strives to create an otherworldly atmosphere. The mysterious lights in the sky hovering over herds of cattle and the electronic music score by Gary Wright generate a science fiction feeling (in many video stores the film is shelved in the science fiction section), and even when the truth of the events is exposed, the explanation seems only slightly less fantastic than the UFO theory proposed by one board member early in the film. Rudolph adds to the sense of ambiguity through constant use of defocused shots that gradually coalesce into a definable image. Perhaps the most effective use of this device occurs near the end, as a line of defused light forms into a row of headlights from the cars of townspeople converging on the secret base where the experiments are being conducted. Rudolph also makes extensive use of rack-focus shots to draw attention to elements in proximity of which the viewer is not at first aware. These shots reinforce the feeling of paranoia by suddenly calling attention to objects or characters in the frame that were not at first visible.

Although these stylistic devices are used to create a sense of unreality, the film is in many ways the most realistic and therefore the least characteristic of Rudolph's films. Yet in this least personal film (and one about the very concept of depersonalization) Rudolph reinforces the importance of human relationships. The violence, paranoia, and sense of randomness overt in this film will become an aspect of his subsequent works, which will become more pronounced in their creation of worlds that have an aura of unreality.

Like *Roadie, Endangered Species* required Rudolph to work within the restrictions of a studio system and resulted in a number of compromises. While Rudolph conformed his own concerns to the demands of a more commercial style of filmmaking, both films received poor distribution because the studios lost confidence in the projects and seemed unsure how to market them. Rudolph claims that the production of *Endangered Species* was shut down after a week of shooting because the studio executives hated the raw, gritty, documentary feel Rudolph and his crew were attempting to achieve (Smith, 69–70). The completed film was given limited distribution and did not play in many parts of the country. Rudolph commented that "it came out of a wasteland where cattle are raised, but since cows do not go to the movies, there were no tickets sold" (Garel, 81). He also stated that these experiences caused him to vow never to work for a studio again, although he would take on more director-for-hire projects a few years later.

RETURN ENGAGEMENT

Rudolph has described *Return Engagement* as "a purge of Hollywood after *Endangered Species*" (Farber, 34). Having worked on two studio projects and been subjected to certain compromises, Rudolph reestablished his position as an independent filmmaker by shooting a documentary in 16mm about Timothy Leary and G. Gordon Liddy. If Rudolph attempted to achieve a documentary quality in *Endangered Species, Return Engagement* was a direct venture into nonfiction film and as such stands apart from Rudolph's other works by the very nature of the genre. Nevertheless, it is easy to see what attracted Rudolph to the subject, as it reflects such already established concerns in the director's work as the nature of success and celebrity in society, the manufacturing of images, and, perhaps most significantly, the conflict between violence and romanticism.

Of all Rudolph's previous work, *Return Engagement* may have closest affinity with *Buffalo Bill and the Indians*. Its two central figures have become cultural icons who seem more than willing to live up to that role in public and reinforce the earlier script's contention that "truth is whatever gets the most applause." Rudolph reinforces their established images through footage of a formal debate between Leary and Liddy, as well as through segments depicting each of them individually and continuing the debate privately. He also incorporates the responses of the public to demonstrate how successfully the images have been manufactured and the roles of representative icons have been established.

Rudolph satirically establishes the position of Liddy and Leary as reflections of the extremes of American culture in the opening shot of Leary playing piano while Liddy sings "America the Beautiful" against the backdrop of an American flag. This introduction is followed by comments from people on the street who seem to know little about the debaters beyond the stereotypical images to which they have been reduced. Throughout the film Rudolph reinforces that the extremities of their positions are reflected in society as a whole. At one point their limo passes a billboard for *Gandhi* (1982) while Liddy discusses having recently seen and enjoyed *Road Warrior* (1981). Liddy is shown working out on a Nautilus machine, while Leary exercises his mind on a word processor (which he directly compares to the Nautilus). As the contrasts are played up, their positions also begin to converge in odd ways. Leary talks to a group of students about how any technology can be used intelligently or stupidly, and there is a cut to Liddy in a firing range using a laser device to improve his aim, followed by another cut to Leary watching video war games being played in an arcade. Liddy finds himself defending Leary to a group of Hell's Angels, who seem to have no objections to the Harvard professor's advocacy of drugs but protest his allegedly having ratted on his associates. Even a party scene at the home of singer Harry Nilsson brings out a cross-section of popular culture, with the guest list including Geraldo Rivera, Arnold Schwarzenegger, and Maria Shriver.

The atmosphere generated in *Endangered Species*—an atmosphere in which anyone is a potential target—is reflected in Liddy's observations to interviewer Carole Hemingway that he would take out anyone who got in the way while he was carrying out actions he believed to be justified. When Hemingway asks if this position would extend to his family, Liddy calmly responds, "You're asking me if there were circumstances under which I would kill my own son, and of course there are." He defends his position with a discourse on man's individual and social natures, which he equates with morality and law. Leary later discusses the social nature of human development and suggests that future social units will be defined by combinations of different intelligences pooling their knowledge.

Whatever validity the ideas of both men may have, the debate scenes suggest that they have packaged their positions into commodities that can be sold to the public in the form of entertainment. Both icons play up to their audience and to each other with lines that seem carefully scripted. The one moment of genuine spontaneity occurs when Leary appears to be momentarily caught off guard by an audience member who claims he was blinded when he was shot in the face by people high on LSD. Offstage, the two debaters momentarily stop their discourse when Liddy's wife (who has often been silent and shown in isolated shots) takes the initiative and begins to discuss women's issues and contemporary morality with Leary's wife. Late in the film, as the two men continue to debate over dinner, they are joined by a journalist who zeroes in on their exploitation of their own images by suggesting that a large percentage of the public considers both of them "consummate scoundrels" and adds that they sound like an old married couple (though this observation hardly constitutes grounds for considering the film in terms of Cavell's remarriage comedies).

Although the two principals are presented as political opposites, the film suggests that such polarity is oversimplified. Leary claims that the difference between the two of them is not left wing or right wing but past and future. Perhaps taking his cue from Leary's support of future generations, Rudolph ends the film with footage of the class to which both men had spoken earlier. The students begin to debate the positions held by the two icons, getting beyond the images and rote recitation of canned lines to discuss the real issues raised by the debate. This scene provides a perfect summation to the film and suggests that while its subjects may be as interested in perpetuating their images as in defining their positions, the issues themselves are still valid.

SONGWRITER

Following his return to independent filmmaking and his own scripts with *Choose Me*, Rudolph took over the directing of *Songwriter*. Although the script was written by Bud Shrake and Rudolph took on the production after filming had started, *Songwriter*, perhaps more than other works of his director-for-hire period, contains stylistic and thematic elements characteristic of his more personal films. The music business setting and the notion of individuals attempting to maintain their independence and integrity in an environment dominated by corporate ideology creates obvious parallels to *Roadie*, as does the Austin, Texas, setting and the generally lighter tone of the film. Yet, as in *Endangered Species*, Rudolph finds within the seeming structure of a familiar genre an opportunity to examine human relationships and to reinforce the importance of family.

The genre in this case is a modern-day western. Musicians Blackie Buck (Kris Kristoferrson) and Doc Jenkins (Willie Nelson) regard themselves as contemporary outlaws, and the territory being contested is their own careers and images. While his desire to gain control of his own music and productions seems to motivate most of Doc's actions (the film was allegedly loosely based on Nelson's own battles in the music industry), Doc's real growth comes about through his realization of the need to "end the party" and recover the home and family he has lost. It is this aspect of the film that connects *Songwriter*, more than any other film of Rudolph's director-for-hire period, to Cavell's concept of the remarriage comedy.

Rudolph establishes the remarriage notion in the extended opening credit sequence, which outlines significant events in Doc's life in a series of quick vignettes (as one critic pointed out, more happens in this credit sequence than happens to many people in their entire lives). The film begins with a characteristic Rudolph opening, a defocused image that slowly sharpens to reveal Doc and Blackie performing on stage behind chicken wire. The reason for the barrier becomes apparent as a beer bottle is thrown into the shot and shatters on the mesh in front of Doc, but the two performers carry on without missing a beat (they obviously know their audience). The almost telepathic understanding between the two friends is established in this first shot and suggests a connection that neither is able to find with the women in their lives. The triangular conflict here does not involve a romantic rivalry but the (nonsexual) understanding that exists between members of the same gender and that exists apart from their relationships with members of the opposite sex. This triangle is confirmed in the next scene with Blackie, Doc, and Doc's first wife, Honey (Melinda Dillon), singing in a recording studio, followed by a cut to Doc and Honey in the back of a car necking while Blackie drives. A further complication is then introduced, in another recording studio shot, as Doc and Blackie harmonize in one room while an obviously pregnant Honey sings in the foreground in another room, separated from them by glass, suggesting that family responsibility is already creating a rift in the happy threesome.

The threesome becomes a twosome, as Doc attempts to settle down to a home life, his domesticity indicated by a set of golf clubs placed prominently in the shot as Doc walks out after a fight with Honey. Quick shots then establish a second marriage, which proves even less successful. In a single cut Doc is shown carrying his new bride over the threshold and then those symbolic golf clubs are being tossed out the door, along with his other belongings, as the second marriage ends. This scene directly echoes Katharine Hepburn's removal of Cary Grant in the 1940 film *The Philadelphia Story* (one of the films Cavell analyzes in *Pursuits of Happiness*) and confirms *Songwriter*'s connection to the conventions of romantic comedy.

The dissolution of his romantic associations would seem to allow for the reestablishment of the professional friendship between Blackie and Doc, but Blackie leaves when Doc decides to sign up with ruthless entrepreneur Rodeo Rocky (played by film director Richard C. Sarafian). As the credits sequence concludes, Blackie comments in a voice-over narration, "In the music business, just like in real life, it's a day to daily war between the sorry and the soulful. And no rule says the righteous gotta win. . . . And when it's all over let 'em say he did it for the love, but he was not above the money."

It is the pursuit of financial success rather than personal satisfaction that seems to have caused Doc's separation from both Blackie and his second wife, Anita (Shannon Wilcox). When Anita arrives at a recording session to find out why she is not receiving her alimony checks (like Honey, she is separated by the glass of a recording studio when she first comes to see Doc), she asks him when he is going to grow up and become a responsible person. Doc responds that he owns his own publishing company and recording studio and asks how responsible he needs to get, suggesting that he associates responsibility with professional success; Anita, however, obviously sees his success as one more means of extending the endless party that has characterized his life on the road and prevented his personal maturation.

Even on a professional level, Doc is criticized for his refusal to conform. As Rodeo Rocky tells him, "You live in some kind of a western fantasy. You ain't Doc Holliday, you're Doc Jenkins," although ironically this observation comes from a streetwise Chicago businessman who is trying to adopt the trappings of the country-music industry by dressing in a Stetson and garish western suit (Doc will later use the historical reference on Rocky after having Blackie and his boys hold the entrepreneur off at gunpoint, while Doc asks him if he has ever heard of the O.K. Corral). Although he has signed with Rocky in an effort to obtain some degree of control over his work, Doc equates the entrepreneur with the system that has oppressed him and therefore regards him as the enemy. The fact that Rocky is an outsider who only dons the western look and, to borrow from Blackie's analogy, is not even in it for the love but strictly for the money adds to his position as a force to be opposed.

A similar position would seem to be held by Blackie's manager Dino (Rip Torn), who is not above his share of dirty tricks to manipulate his contractees. Still, Dino is depicted as an insider and earns the begrudging admiration of Blackie and Doc because he plays by the same set of rules as they do. Even before he joins forces with them to oppose Rocky, a connection is established between Doc and Dino in a quick shot of Dino returning home and kissing his wife and baby before going into the bedroom to get a gun, indicating that, like Doc, he faces a conflict between his quiet home life and his violent professional one.

Dino is hoping to promote his new find, Gilda (Lesley Ann Warren), a raw and insecure singer but one in whom Doc sees an obvious talent. Despite being under the control of Dino, Doc takes an interest (albeit strictly professional) in her career and begins to work with her. His association with Gilda, although a part of his business arrangements, also awakens in him (as Anita or even Honey could not) an awareness of the sacrifices made in the name of career. He does not immediately associate this with himself, however, and he tells Gilda (who has a boyfriend) about Honey having to give up her career when she started a family. Rudolph slowly moves from a two-shot to a close-up of Doc as he talks, as though the discussion of Honey and family is rekindling a desire for a return to a domestic life and an awareness of what he has lost.

A short time later Doc tries to reestablish his relationship with Honey, appearing at her door in the guise of a vacuum cleaner sales-man (a choice that combines the notions of professionalism and domesticity). She immediately picks up on the charade, and they indulge in the kind of good-natured banter that suggests the shared understanding of earlier couples in the films identified by Cavell as remarriage comedies. This leads to a more serious discourse about the nature of their relationship, as Honey tells Doc to stop trying to outdo the Fortune 500 and just be a poet. The Cavellian concept of a past life that must be recovered surfaces, as Honey reminds Doc that he used to talk about following an artistic vision. Honey equates this loss of an artistic vision with a change in both Doc and the music industry as a whole. She acknowledges the effect of commerce on art (a major Rudolph concern and one that will be most directly addressed in *The Moderns*) when she comments that "the bankers own all the art and the artists don't think about anything but money." In response, Doc demonstrates that he has not lost his personal integrity by playing her a song he has written (which itself presents the conflict between nostalgic imagery and commercial gain with the recurring line "Who'll buy my memories?"). The camera stays largely on Doc as he sings, cutting only briefly to a family photo col-lage. Doc tries to convince Honey that they should get back together, but she responds that if he gets tired of partying she and the girls will be there, implying that it is he who will have to return to her. When the girls return home, Doc sits with them on the floor as they practice the guitar, and the camera pulls back discretely from the intimate scene to include Honey, who is watching from the couch, the composition uniting the entire family in a single frame but still maintaining a sense of distance between Doc and Honey.

This domestic scene, perhaps more than any other in the film, demonstrates *Songwriter*'s affinity with the comedies of remarriage. Honey's house takes on the function of the green world and provides Doc with his only refuge from the problems of the music business.

The dialogue between Doc and Honey when he first shows up at her doorstep (and is adopting another role, as do many of the characters in the films Cavell has identified) demonstrates their shared language, and it is the rediscovery of this communication that sets in motion their inevitable reconciliation. Ironically, Doc also shares a level of private communication with Blackie, as demonstrated by the convoluted conversation they have when Blackie corners Doc about why he is putting Gilda's name on the songs and not his. The two punctuate each other's arguments with the same repeated phrases that suggest a shared understanding, even when each admits that the conversation is making little sense. The shared communication between Doc and Blackie is one that they will undoubtedly never lose. Doc must learn that his shared language with Honey is equally important, however, and that their relationship ultimately provides a different type of personal fulfillment than his association with Blackie.

As Doc makes an effort to recapture his past family life, he also takes steps toward gaining greater independence in his professional life. He burns down his office and sets up a new pirate company. He also arranges to publish his songs under Gilda's name so Rocky cannot collect on him. At the same time, he begins training Gilda as a singer and performer. In one particularly sensual moment he goes into the recording booth to help her through one passage of a song and their duet takes on an erotic quality, as he first stands behind and then facing her. Despite the undercurrents in this scene, Doc seems interested in using any sexual attraction between them only to build Gilda's self-confidence. When Gilda later attempts to seduce Doc in his hotel room, he discourages her advances. In a variation on a scene in *Welcome to L.A.,* the phone rings and she asks him not to answer, but Doc does and tells her it is Honey calling. After Gilda leaves, it is revealed that it is actually Blackie on the other end, but whether Blackie or Honey, the point has been made to Gilda that she faces insurmountable competition for Doc's affections.

Gilda responds to the rejection by going to Honey's house to apologize and takes an overdose of pills while in the bathroom. Although Doc has already indicated to Blackie during the hotel room scene that he has given up partying to focus on his songwriting, Gilda's suicide attempt becomes the final motivating factor in his journey to responsibility. He clears everyone out of his house and then sits down to continue working on his music. Doc's song carries over to a shot of him driving to Honey's house to tell her the party is over and then driving away.

With the party ended, Doc still has to straighten out his professional problems, and he and Blackie take to the road again to bring an end to his association with Rodeo Rocky. Doc's "salvation" comes from Gilda, who, of all the characters, finally finds a way to balance her personal and professional motivations by getting married, finding religion, and deciding to devote her talents to singing gospel music as a career. This comes, of course, after Doc has gotten out of his contract with Rocky and has sold Gilda's contract to him for a sizable sum. Even Dino comes out ahead by robbing the box office. Doc maintains his integrity in a final gesture by leaving Rocky with one last, presumably successful, song. He and Dino converge on a set of ramps outside the auditorium (in a composition Rudolph had used in *Roadie,* when Travis asserts his independence by leaving Lola behind at the Alice Cooper concert), and Doc is last seen in a car with Honey and the kids. As he and his family drive away, Blackie, who has been coupled with a succession of groupies throughout the film, appears to have entered, at least temporarily, into a commitment with Doc's secretary, and the two of them embrace in an empty auditorium. A far cry from the rowdy opening performance shot of Doc and Blackie, the two outlaws now appear willing to settle for more stable and sedate relationships.

These final domestic images of Blackie and Doc reestablish Rudolph's belief in romance as the ultimate goal of his characters. As such, the film has clear connections to *Choose Me,* which directly preceeded it, while the attack on those who seek to control individual talent for profit anticipates *Trouble in Mind* and *The Moderns.* Once again Rudolph demonstrated an ability to adapt his own interests and visual look to the linear demands of a narrative script, but the film was another victim of poor distribution. Some critics, most notably Pauline Kael, even used their reviews to attack the studio for its lack of faith in the film. Although Rudolph has expressed objections to the handling of his early studio-generated projects, his next director-for-hire production would be the source of his greatest frustration in dealing with a studio.

MADE IN HEAVEN

Despite the difficulties Rudolph had with the studio over the final cut of *Made in Heaven,* the film as released draws on the vision Rudolph had developed in *Choose Me* and *Trouble in Mind* and contains touches

that are unmistakably Rudolph's. The film once again works a variation on the remarriage formula (with the ultimate "green world" in
the genre, heaven itself) and incorporates music and musicians as key
elements. In addition, the film anticipates *The Moderns* in its consideration of the conflict between artistry and commerce.

Made in Heaven employs the conventions of the spiritual fantasy
films that were common during World War II, such as *Here Comes Mr.
Jordan* (1941), *A Guy Named Joe* (1943), and *Stairway to Heaven* (1946).
The story actually begins in postwar America, a time in which such
film fantasies were being replaced by a move toward greater realism.
While the conditions of war had been an obvious factor in generating
works that provided a romanticized view of an afterlife, the genre
interestingly resurfaced in the late 1970s, with films like *Heaven Can
Wait* (a 1978 remake of *Mr. Jordan*), and a series of reincarnation
comedies. The trend has continued in more recent works, such as
Field of Dreams (1984) and *Ghost* (1990). The reemergence of the
genre in contemporary times seems to be a response not to any specific social conditions but to a desire for a reaffirmation of spirituality
in a society where concepts of morality are no longer as easily defined
as in previous generations (or at least as reflected in the movies
embraced by those generations). In keeping with this sense of moral
ambiguity, Rudolph presents a heaven that is not without its dark side,
as well as a depiction of modern society in which romantic love seems
as much a matter of chance as a result of some divine plan.

The contrast between Hollywood romanticism and the difficulty
of achieving it in reality is established in the opening scenes (shot in
black and white), as Mike (Timothy Hutton) and his girlfriend watch
Hitchcock's 1946 film *Notorious* in a theater. Though not directly
representative of the afterlife genre, the Hitchcock film provides a
reference point to the direction Mike's story will take in its depiction
of the sacrifices that have to be made by its lovers. For much of the
film Cary Grant and Ingrid Bergman are actually separated (albeit by
political rather than divine intervention), and she is in fact married to
some one else, as Mike's heavenly lover will be for a time during her
return to earth.

After leaving the theater it is revealed (in another of Rudolph's
Hopperesque café scenes) that Mike has lost his job. He is unable to
get another at a bank because of his independence and his contempt
for the blatant pursuit of wealth. He is also about to lose his girlfriend, as he discovers when she tells him that she has agreed to
marry another (the camera zooming slowly in to the car window as

Mike tries to convince his lover to go to California with him and then stopping when she breaks the news to him). Mike decides to head for California alone, but he does not get far from home when he stops to rescue two kids trapped in a car in a lake and drowns.

Mike is greeted on his arrival in heaven by his aunt (Maureen Stapleton), who indoctrinates him into the rules of his surroundings. Prior to the aunt's appearance, the shot briefly fades to a child playing jazz piano, setting up the important music motif and demonstrating the ethereal nature of things in heaven. Stapleton takes Mike to her quarters (which have an ever-changing view outside the picture window), where she has taken up painting—something she was unable to do on earth. The implication is that one major aspect of the afterlife is artistic pursuit, even for those who had no particular artistic facility on earth.

Mike soon gets oriented toward life in heaven and the ability to move from one location to another simply by imagining where he wants to be. Interestingly, he and the other inhabitants of heaven cast reflections in mirrors, which, given the function of these objects in previous Rudolph films, suggests that the search for identity continues after death, as Mike will discover when he learns that those who are in heaven will return to earth, presumably to continue the process of self-discovery. Another intriguing variation that Rudolph provides on the afterlife genre (with the help of his longtime collaborators, photographer Jan Kiesser and art director Steven Legler) is his depiction of a heaven that is not always whiteness and sunshine, as demonstrated in one surprisingly ominous view of kids playing on a dark street where Mike gets his first glimpse of the backlit, cigarette-smoking Emmett (played, in a weirdly androgynous performance, by an unbilled Debra Winger).

During his initial exploration of heaven, Mike also encounters Annie Packert (Kelly McGillis), whose first appearance at a piano recalls the small child briefly glimpsed on Mike's arrival. Annie was born in heaven (establishing the intriguing concept of a sexual afterlife) and is a "new soul." She and Mike begin a relationship as he learns from her about heaven, while she continually questions him about earth. His past life is acknowledged when he revisits the house in which he grew up (which contains a television set that seems curiously anachronistic, as Mike has apparently died in 1946), and while there he finds his mirrored reflection is that of a child, which may be the one he was once or the one he is soon to become.

In *Made in Heaven* (1987), Annie (Kelly McGillis) and Mike (Timothy Hutton) discuss their impending wedding in heaven with an angel (John Considine). While the wings reflect the traditional depiction of ethereal beings, the use of a top hat and coat rather than flowing robes indicate Rudolph's variations on the conventions of fantasy films.
Courtesy Museum of Modern Art/Film Stills Archive.

If the previous black-and-white earth scenes had an Edward Hopper quality, heaven proves to be pure Maxfield Parrish, particularly in a shot of Annie sitting on a bed that is floating above a lake. Eventually the romance between Mike and Annie becomes physical, leading to a free-floating love scene that recalls Ken Russell's *Women in Love* (1969). Mike begins to build his dream house, finding he can reconstruct it at will, and makes plans to wed Annie, although she reminds him that according to heaven they already are married. As the wedding is about to take place, however, Annie fades out, to be replaced by Emmett, who informs Mike that she has been sent to be born on earth. Mike corners Emmett (who is found watching a group of dancers, establishing another motif that will become significant later in the film) and tries to convince the supervisor to let him return to earth as well. Emmett finally agrees but tells Mike he has a limited time to reunite with Annie, although he changes the terms as the conversation continues, and ends up giving Mike 30 years to find her.

The second part of the film deals with the experiences of the two principals on earth. Although some critics objected that these scenes feel rather shapeless and unfocused, this might be regarded as a deliberate contrast to the perfection of heaven and an indication of the random quality of life. The earth sequence also serves to demonstrate that the love of the two leads, while easy to achieve in heaven, is much harder to accomplish on earth. Not only do fate and chance influence earthly relationships, but Rudolph's characters, like many in his previous films, also find themselves confronted by other pressures. Mike seeks some sense of his own identity, whereas Annie finds her relationships challenged by problems of career and success.

The quest by Mike, rechristened Elmo when he is reborn, becomes not only an attempt to reunite with Annie (who is now Ally Chandler) but also a search for artistic fulfillment. Although he shows an interest in the piano at an early age, his talents are suppressed because of his mother's loutish boyfriend. Ally, who had been associated with the piano in heaven, finds other artistic outlets on earth, first by assisting her ex-serviceman father when he becomes a toymaker and later as the author of a book about her imaginary friend Mike.

In an anticipation of *The Moderns,* Rudolph uses the earth sequences to comment on the conflict between art and commerce. Ally marries a film student (they first meet when he asks directions to a class being taught by a professor with the same name as one of Mike's friends in heaven) who becomes successful as a director of commercials. He is unable to reconcile Ally's true artistic ability with his own commercial success, however, and, although she claims she will change for him, he admits that he cannot keep up with her and they divorce. She later begins a relationship with another man (after surprising him in a shower while touring a house), but by now she has begun to feel a link to Mike, even though she has not yet met him on earth.

Mike/Elmo, in the meantime, goes through a period of aimless wandering. Like Coop in *Trouble In Mind* he drifts briefly into a life of crime when coerced by a female Lucifer (appropriately named Lucille) who appears in a red dress at a garage where Elmo takes his car when it breaks down. Recalling the Mephistophelian role of Solo in *Trouble in Mind,* Lucille takes Elmo to a roadhouse (where the band plays "Up Jumped the Devil") and implicates him in a robbery, although, unlike Coop, he goes along with the scheme because he naively believes their target has been fleecing Lucille's mother. Once in her car, Lucille kisses Elmo and then pulls a gun on him and tells him to get out.

To counteract his encounter with Lucille, Emmett briefly appears to Elmo at a roadside to try to get him back on track (although Elmo has no recollection of his previous existence). In one of the most blatant pieces of symbolism in all of Rudolph's work, Elmo sprawls on the highway in a crucifixion image and the shot dissolves to Ally's eyes, indicating that she is the object of his redemption and resurrection. As with other Rudolph characters who have a telepathic connection, the two share a dream of each other, after which Elmo awakens and looks at his disheveled reflection in the mirror. The shared dream not only confirms the connection between the two characters but suggests that their positions are reversing. Elmo begins to discover his true nature, culminating in a musical career, while Ally momentarily experiences a period of aimlessness (when she awakens from the dream she is revealed to be in a jail after having gone on a drinking binge).

Ironically, Elmo's musical destiny, which was temporarily denied by one set of "parents," is restored by his encounter with another—a meeting that allows him a brief (if unrecognized) reconciliation with his past life. In one of the film's most poignant moments, he is picked up while hitchhiking by the parents he had in his previous existence on earth as Mike. During their drive, Mike's mother secretly confides to him that she is dying. She also tells him about the son she lost and how, after forgetting one day and setting a place for him at the dinner table, she had a premonition that he was all right. As they are preparing to part, his father gives him a trumpet he saw Elmo admiring in the window of a pawnshop. This gift from the father (a concept that has an obvious spiritual connotation) becomes the means by which Elmo can fulfill his artistic destiny. As if to add further reinforcement to the concept of artistic fulfillment as a heavenly gift, spiritual intervention again occurs when, while driving drunk, Elmo spins his car out of control and winds up in front of a gallery displaying one of the paintings his aunt made in heaven.

As Elmo is coming to terms with his former parents, Ally loses the only father she has ever had and inherits his company. The parallelism of their lives continues, as Elmo forms a band from a group of street musicians and makes a record deal with a promoter from the Halo label (who is one of the people he met while in heaven). Rudolph depicts the recording of the album in some detail, recalling the fascination he has shown for the collaborative process of music recording

in *Welcome to L.A.* and *Songwriter.* Although the album gains Elmo
visibility, including television interviews, his success, like that of Ally
earlier with her book, does not result in the reconciliation of the two
lovers. Rather, these pursuits reflect the personal fulfillment each
must find before they can find each other. When that reconciliation
finally occurs, it seems more a matter of coincidence and comes
down to a shared glance on a crowded street. At first Elmo appears to
have lost, as he briefly returns to heaven to face Emmett, but he is
returned to earth, and he and Ally are last shown dancing in an
empty ballroom—an image that recalls the tentative positivism at the
end of *Songwriter.*

In an interview in *Film Comment,* Rudolph indicated that the
ending as originally conceived and shot was a good deal more elaborate and complex. The studio objected to the darker elements in the
latter part of the film, however, and the ending was recut against the
director's wishes. As Rudolph stated, "The ending was brilliant, the
best shooting I ever did, and it was all cut out. It was the only reason
I did the film. I said, 'I'll shoot your schmaltz, but the audience is
gonna have to pay for it, it can't all be this light.' And the second half
of the film was very dark and very funny. And most of that went"
(Smith, 65).

In Rudolph's cut, just as the two lovers finally see each other, Elmo
is hit by a limo driven by the mechanic at the garage where Elmo first
encountered Lucille (who is in the limo's back seat). During one
uninterrupted take, Ally reaches down to touch him and as the camera pulls back she is gone and the street is empty. Continuing the shot,
Lucille comes to claim the body, but in a puff of smoke she is replaced
by Emmett. As the camera tilts up to Elmo, a hand reaches for him
that turns out to belong to Ally. Elmo wakes up in heaven and is told
by Emmett that his time ran out but that, "If it's love, it won't matter."
The film ends with Elmo walking into a nightclub where all the cast
members are gathered and finding Ally, with whom he begins to
dance. As released, the film seems incomplete and unsatisfying, with
no explanation given for Emmett's decision to return Elmo to Earth.
The cutting of Lucille from the ending of the film also leaves her
character undefined. In the released version she seems a momentary
temptation (and a rather ineffectual one) in Elmo's quest, whereas the
original ending would have connected her directly to the relationship
of the two lovers and in contrast to Emmett.

In addition to confusion generated by the abrupt ending, critics
objected to the structure of the film, particularly the second half,

which splits the focus between the two principals. These objections may in part stem from the variations Rudolph works on the remarriage formula. Whereas the traditional genre structure depends on a couple who have to relearn to love each other, and consequently much of the actions depends on their interaction and the knowledge they gain from each other, Rudolph presents his lovers as having perfected their relationship in heaven and now having to "find themselves" (to use a popular contemporary phrase) in their earthly existence before they can return to that relationship. The philosophical/epistemological inquiry experienced by the couples discussed by Cavell here becomes equated with artistic development, which has already been depicted in the sequences in heaven as an indication of spiritual fulfillment.

The seeming aimlessness of the later scenes, particularly those involving Elmo, provide another example of the director's view of contemporary society. Just as the afterlife films have resurfaced in contemporary cinema in response to a need for some sense of spirituality that goes beyond outmoded notions of traditional religious doctrine, Rudolph's characters appear to be searching for something that will give their lives meaning in a world in which morality is an ambiguous concept and success is not necessarily equated with personal fulfillment. In Rudolph's vision, this fulfillment comes through artistic achievement and at least the possibility of perfect romance. While the attainment of the latter is a concern of all of Rudolph's films, his next film, *The Moderns,* suggested that artistic achievement could be subverted by commercialization.

MORTAL THOUGHTS

If Rudolph was required to remove the darker elements of *Made in Heaven,* it was precisely this aspect of his worldview that was necessary for *Mortal Thoughts,* another project with which he became involved after filming had begun. But once again Rudolph was able to adapt the material to his visual style. While more plot-dependent than many of the director's films, *Mortal Thoughts* provided Rudolph with an opportunity to continue his experiments with viewpoint, and in fact the issue of viewpoint becomes an essential part of the narrative. In this case viewpoint reinforces a favorite Rudolph concern: the ambiguous nature of reality.

The genre territory is the suspense thriller, specifically Hitchcock's *Strangers on a Train* (1951) by way of Clouzot's *Diabolique* (1955). The plot involves two women, Cynthia (Demi Moore) and Joyce (Glenne Headley) who conspire to cover up the murder of Joyce's loutish husband, James (Bruce Willis). In typical noir fashion, the conspiracy creates a strain on the two participants, as each becomes concerned that the other will expose the truth. The events are presented through a framing device involving the police interrogation of Cynthia by detective John Wood (Harvey Keitel) and Linda Nealon (Billie Neal), limiting us to Cynthia's presentation and interpretation of what has taken place. In the finale, a new interpretation is provided, although the viewpoint remains Cynthia's, and calls into question whether we can believe any of the interpretations provided.

A bond between the two women is established in home-movie footage of the two as little girls, which is used to break up the opening credits. These images from the past have a soft-focused, unreal quality, and Rudolph continues to disorient the viewer's sense of reality in the first appearance of Moore at the police station, as she is seen through a set of venetian blinds moving in slow motion. As she disappears behind a partition and reemerges, the film goes to normal speed. The conflict between image and reality is further demonstrated in the use of a video camera during the interrogations, with Cynthia seen on the monitor at significant points in her testimony.

The connection between Cynthia and Joyce is reinforced as Cynthia's testimony leads into the first flashback of Joyce's wedding. While being interrogated, Cynthia fiddles with her wedding ring, and when the flashback begins the camera tilts down to the band and then dissolves to one of Rudolph's familiar soft-focused shots, which sharpens on a set of lights. The camera again tilts down to a band playing at the wedding (the transition playing on the visual pun of wedding band) and is followed shortly by a cut from a shot of James to a close-up of Joyce's hand with her new wedding ring. As the camera tilts up to Joyce's face, Cynthia is revealed to be standing behind her. Throughout the wedding scene, Rudolph provides shots of Cynthia watching the couple from a distance or framed between them as they argue over money they have been given as a wedding gift.

This triangular construction continues in a scene in Joyce's beauty parlor (the Clip 'N' Dye) when James again comes in search of money, looting the cash register and leaving their baby with Joyce. The two fight, and Cynthia tries to intervene. The first hint of separation between the two friends is provided as James leaves, and Joyce, in close-up, threatens to kill him and turn half the business over to Cynthia. The camera pans over to isolate Cynthia and her repeat of the threatening remark is overlapped on the soundtrack, followed by a cut to Cynthia on the monitor in the police station as she finishes describing the incident to the police.

Soon after, Joyce gives indications of making good her threat. She comes into the beauty parlor with rat poison, which she mixes with the sugar being taken to James for his coffee. As Joyce carries the bowl up to their apartment above the beauty parlor, Rudolph provides a Hitchcockian shot that keeps the focus on the sugar bowl. Cynthia again intervenes, this time to save James (and indirectly Joyce, who will be charged with murder), and Rudolph continues to emphasize the sugar bowl as they talk. Although Cynthia succeeds in upsetting the sugar bowl before James can use any of it, he makes sexual advances to her, and she has to fight him off.

Both the triangular configurations and the Hitchcock references surface in the murder scene. The two women decide to have a night out, and as they drive to an amusement park in Joyce's van, James suddenly pops up between them. His sexual preoccupation with both women is demonstrated by a pan from a two-shot of James with

In *Mortal Thoughts* (1991), James (Bruce Willis) makes the fatal mistake of accompanying Cynthia (Demi Moore, left) and Joyce (Glenne Headly) to an amusement park. Throughout the drive to the park Rudolph makes selective use of framing to isolate James with each of the women.
Courtesy Museum of Modern Art/Film Stills Archive.

his head on Joyce's shoulder to a two-shot encompassing James and Cynthia while he implies that he is going to make advances to her. In a complex shot, Rudolph pans from a close-up of Cynthia to a close-up of Joyce and then back, but the shot ends on a close-up of Wood interrogating Cynthia. Once at the fairgrounds, Joyce and James go through a reiteration of their arguments about money, and fight over the keys to the van.

The fairground scenes, in addition to providing echoes of Hitch-cock's *Strangers on a Train,* offer the first indications that Cynthia's story may not be the truth. Her potential distortion is implied by the increasingly distorted images of the carnival. The camera angles become tilted and the imagery more dreamlike (stylistic choices that appear to be motivated by more than just James's having snorted cocaine, as the shots do not appear to be strictly from his point of view). The air of unreality is reinforced by a strange double exposure shot of the Ferris wheel against the moon, with each object seeming to cross the visual plane of the other. As if to emphasize the unreality of Cynthia's testimony, Rudolph dissolves from the Ferris wheel shot to a close-up of Cynthia on the video monitor as she is interrogated in the police station.

After Joyce shows Cynthia James's body in the back of the van and tells her she cut his throat with a utility knife while they were fight-ing, Rudolph keeps the two women isolated in separate shots, demonstrating the rift between them that is already developing as a result of the murder. Only after they stop to look at the body (the point at which their conspiracy begins) are they shown in a two-shot, and once they begin preparing their story Rudolph returns to alternating close-ups. The women are again shown in the same shot as they dispose of the body, but the sense of unreality returns through the use of slow motion.

The effect of the murder on the bond between Cynthia and Joyce is paralleled by the impact it has on Cynthia's relationship with her husband, Arthur (John Pankow). When they part after dumping James's body, the two women embrace as Joyce comments that they are friends forever and will look out for each other. During this scene Joyce is facing away from the camera, so although it is a two-shot, only Cynthia's face is visible. The composition is repeated a short time later when Cynthia returns home and embraces Arthur before telling him what happened. As with the shots of the two women, Rudolph composes the scene between Cynthia and her husband so that they are seldom in the same shot together, or at least not in the same plane (at one point she sits on the couch in the background, while Arthur stands in the foreground). This visual alienation in reinforced verbally, as they begin to misunderstand each other during their conversation, indicating that their shared communication is breaking down.

Once the conspiracy begins, Rudolph continues to emphasize the separation of the two women. Cynthia takes the van to be cleaned, and the distorted angles and slow motion of the fairground scenes are again employed, along with subliminal shots of James writhing on the floor, which provide a clue to what really happened, as Cynthia allegedly did not witness the murder. The motivation for her distortion of the truth is also provided in shots of her baby in a stroller as she cleans the van.

The two women do not interact directly again until James's funeral, where they sneak off to the powder room together to conspire on their story. During this scene Rudolph makes use of characteristic devices, including a shot of Joyce reflected in multiple mirrors as she lies to Cynthia about not talking to a co-worker. Rudolph also focuses prominently on a painting of a fallen angel when Cynthia tries to encourage Joyce to continue the deception by telling her she is a terrific liar but has just lost confidence in herself. Cynthia's contention that Joyce is beginning to crack is reinforced when the women are alone in the beauty parlor and Joyce claims she hears James's voice (during which Rudolph inserts a quick shot of the two of them at their wedding). Rudolph ends the beauty parlor scene with a shot of two gold-plated female heads being used as wig stands in a window display, once again reinforcing both an atmosphere that things are not what they seem and the undercurrent of a male-dominated society in which women are used as objects or treated as incomplete beings.

Joyce convinces Cynthia to take a bag containing James's jewelry and his gun. In another Hitchcockian shot echoing the earlier scene with the sugar bowl, Rudolph keeps the bag prominent in the shot as Cynthia's daughter looks inside while Cynthia and Arthur argue. Cynthia is able to prevent Arthur from finding out what is in the bag by telling him it is her tampons, knowing that this is the one alibi she can provide that a man will not pursue.

Following a suicide attempt, Joyce is briefly detained in jail, and Cynthia comes to see her. Rudolph reinforces their separation through alternating close-ups and the use of the cell bars, which keep them apart even in two-shots. The alienation of Cynthia and Arthur also becomes more direct, as he tells her that if she is still involved with Joyce she should pack her bags and go with her. Later, as the two argue about getting a divorce, Arthur tells Cynthia, "I'm sick of you favoring her over me, Cynthia. You always did. All these years you haven't been married to me. You two have been married to each other. Well, now you can have her with my blessings." In a decision that defeats her alleged motivation for the conspiracy, Arthur also tells her he is taking the kids because he does not consider her a fit mother. As Cynthia finishes describing the scene during her interrogation, Wood points out that she and Arthur are beginning to sound like Joyce and James.

After Joyce discovers from a phone conversation with Cynthia that Arthur is alone, he is murdered, and Joyce is the logical suspect. It is at this point that detective Wood begins to suspect Cynthia's account of events, particularly because she so readily provided Joyce with an opportunity to kill Arthur, even though she believed Joyce was becoming paranoid and potentially dangerous. Although he begins to suspect the truth, he allows Cynthia to leave, and as she exits Joyce is brought in for interrogation. While Joyce sits in her car, reflected Christmas lights cause Cynthia to recall the lights of the fairground, and, in a characteristic image of self-reflection and introspection, Rudolph zooms in to a close-up of her eyes in the rearview mirror. The alleged truth unfolds in a flashback, and it is revealed that Cynthia actually stabbed James when he tried to rape her. Even with this change in perspective, Rudolph indicates that the events still alienate the two women, as he again alternates close-ups of them in the flashback scenes after the body is found. A shot in the van with both of them visible emphasizes the distance between them, and it occurs at the point at which Joyce decides not to drive to the hospital. Although Cynthia's original distortion seems to have been designed to protect herself, this action returns the burden of guilt to Joyce by implying that she allowed James to die when it might have been possible to save him. As the flashback ends, Cynthia returns to the police station and prepares to offer new testimony, but the use of slow motion and the final shot of her on the TV monitor once again implies that perceptions of what is real cannot be easily determined.

In presenting this final flashback, Rudolph implies that even this may not be the truth, as the scenes of Cynthia's recollection employ the distorted camera angles and sound used for the earlier depiction of the murder, which create an atmosphere of unreality. Given that Cynthia is alone during this final flashback, the distortions raise the question of why she would lie to herself. The most likely answer for her self-deception is that she actually wanted to kill James, and perhaps by extension her own husband, whether in fact she did or not. The motivation may have been her perception that James was creating a rift in her friendship with Joyce—a conclusion that is supported by her choosing to begin her recollections with their wedding. Arthur's decision to take their children also provides the motivation for his elimination. Such a reading calls into question all of the events we have witnessed from her perspective. For example, although she makes herself out to be the heroine in the sugar bowl incident, it is just as likely that she, rather than Joyce, may have instigated it but then was unable to carry it out. Cynthia's self-deception also raises doubts about what actually happened to Arthur and her role in these events.

This ending requires reevaluation of Cynthia's entire testimony and leaves unanswered what really occurred with regard to Arthur's death. While it might be concluded that Joyce still committed this murder, even if she was not the one who stabbed James, the motivations becomes less clear. Detective Wood suggests that Cynthia had

Detectives John Wood (Harvey Keitel) and Linda Nealon (Billie Neal) interrogate Cynthia (Demi Moore) about her involvement in James's murder. As in *Remember My Name*, the bars on the window imply the heroine's entrapment. Courtesy Museum of Modern Art/Film Stills Archive.

no reason to fear for Arthur's life because Joyce had not committed the first murder, but this only raises further questions about why she would commit this one. It could be seen as a means of protecting Cynthia, as Arthur knew the truth, or as an act of revenge for Cynthia's killing of James. The echoes of *Strangers on a Train* also raise the disturbing possibility that the women may have exchanged murders like the protagonists of Hitchcock's film as a means of escaping from their bad marriages.

Mortal Thoughts was released a few months before *Thelma and Louise* (1991), causing some critics to draw comparisons between the two films. However, whereas the self-defense killing of a rapist in the later film actually helped to bond the two women in their opposition to male authority, the murder in *Mortal Thoughts,* no matter what the truth, brings about a disintegration of the relationship between the two female protagonists. While both women face pressure from their husbands about their friendship (Arthur in particular seems to object to Joyce because he regards her as from a lower social class), this seems to strengthen the unity between the two women, and their dissociation only occurs when their husbands have been eliminated. The bond between the two women—which, as the home-movie footage implies, was developed in childhood—appears to be stronger than either of their marriages. Although Cynthia's relationship with Arthur seems less obviously troubled than Joyce's with James, there are implications even in the early scenes that Arthur's preoccupation with his career is creating some strain. This obsession with career ironically seems to be motivated by a desire to avoid the financial pressures that are causing dissension between Joyce and James. At least there are occasional hints of a raw sexuality in the relationship between Joyce and James that presumably accounts for their attraction, while the marriage of Cynthia and Arthur seems sterile and devoid of emotion of any kind, even anger.

Rather than attempting some form of reconciliation, Joyce (and later Cynthia) is willing to acknowledge the inevitable disintegration of her marriage. Joyce makes no secret of her desire to kill James (at least if we are to believe any of Cynthia's testimony), and after his death she begins to emphasize her enigmatic qualities. When she finally shows up at Cynthia's to recover the gun, she has taken to wrapping her face in a scarf, and Arthur jokes, "I thought you was Greta Garbo there for a minute." Even more enigmatic, however, is Cynthia, as she controls the viewpoint throughout the film, and her final recollections call into question everything that has gone before.

The final voice-over comment—"Ready? Let's get started"—indicates that we will not find out what really occurred. While the ending becomes the ultimate extension of the inability to determine the reality that Rudolph has carefully developed, the film provides some further insights into the director's worldview. The violence that has been present in much of his work is here taken to extremes and leaves no apparent redemption for these characters, even if such actions may be justified (and, given our inability to determine what actually happened, there is no evidence that they are). In this sense the film is closest in spirit to *Remember My Name* and *Trouble in Mind:* it draws from the first film a sense of women asserting control in response to unsuccessful relationships and shares the second's environment in which women are alienated by the actions of men. Like both earlier films, *Mortal Thoughts* emphasizes the concepts of entrapment and claustrophobia—from the overcrowded beauty parlor and apartment above it to the police station where Cynthia's interrogation by Wood becomes another form of entrapment. Joyce and Cynthia are involved in relationships in which they are shown to be dominated, and even after the elimination of their husbands this male domination continues, demonstrated most directly in the cat-and-mouse game Wood plays while questioning Cynthia (occasionally winking at his female co-worker to demonstrate his control of the situation).

Unlike his other films, *Mortal Thoughts* does not provide the possibility of romance, either in or out of the marriage state. This decidedly bleak conception would carry over to Rudolph's return to a more personal project with his next film, *Equinox,* and if the characters in that film ultimately are provided with some possibility for redemption, it comes at a greater price and in an environment that is more oppressive than anything the director has yet put on film. Acknowledging the darker atmosphere of both films, the director observed that *Equinox* is "a gritty movie about improbable things. The same sense of contradiction was felt in *Mortal Thoughts,* which is basically an anti-love story. *Mortal Thoughts* is very violent on one level because it's about what our society has really done to married couples. We have this attitude of 'I love you, I love you, I love you, so let's get married and then we won't have to deal with it anymore.' So the movie is a love story about people who hate each other, and its disguised as a kind of thriller" (Brooks, 60-61).

Ironically, for a film whose ending provides Rudolph's most radical subversion yet of the logic of film structure, *Mortal Thoughts* was regarded as a work that finally demonstrated that the director could adapt his unique qualities to a more conventional project. The finale, rather than being seen as a deconstruction of filmic reality, was viewed simply as a twist ending that presumably revealed the truth (an interpretation that disregards how the same distorting elements used in Cynthia's flashback were employed in the initial murder scene). Rudolph has indicated that it was probably the only one of his films to make money. He also noted that once again the studio attempted to tamper with the ending, particularly after stars Willis and Moore had success with *Die Hard 2* (1990) and *Ghost* (1990), respectively. Among other things, there were discussions of reshooting, with a romance created for James and Cynthia, as well as an ending in which James would not be dead but would come back to try to kill the two women. Fortunately, Rudolph had the support of star Moore, who was also one of the film's co-producers, and they were able to preserve the integrity of the film.

While all of his director-for-hire projects contain points of interest and connections to his more personal work, *Mortal Thoughts* demonstrated that the director had found a way to be mainstream and artistically radical at the same time. Even the obvious product placement for Dunkin' Donuts is taken to such ludicrous extremes that it appears to be a deliberate attempt on the director's part to satirize the demands of commercial filmmaking (Rudolph once stated, "One thing you won't find in my movies, I hope, are any ringing endorsements of any commerical products" [Smith, 63]). *Mortal Thoughts* suggests a new direction for Rudolph's work—one in which he will be able to express his individuality within the restrictions of mainstream studio production.

CHAPTER 10

Mrs. Parker and the Vicious Circle: Into Love and Out Again

Women, despite the fact that nine out of ten of them go through life with a death-bed air either of snatching-the-last-moment or with martyr resignation, do not die tomorrow—or the next day. They have to live on to any one of many bitter ends.

—Zelda Fitzgerald, "Eulogy on the Flapper" (1922)

Mrs. Parker and the Vicious Circle (1994) in many ways brings Alan Rudolph's career full circle. In addition to reuniting Rudolph with Robert Altman after 15 years, the film returns to the construction of *Welcome to L.A.,* with the examination of triangular relationships among a large group of characters. Even more than that first collaboration, the film has the feeling of an Altmanesque party, particularly in the depiction of the Algonquin Round Table. Yet, as the title implies, the focus is split between that group and one of its principal members, and in its depiction of the heroine the film deals with themes that are characteristically Rudolph's. For all its connections to past work, however, the film also represents new directions in Rudolph's films, not only in the historical fidelity of its content but in the stylistic use of a widescreen aspect ratio and long takes.

Thematically, *Mrs. Parker* appears to be most closely related to *The Moderns,* as it deals with historical figures at roughly the same time period. But whereas the earlier film took a myth-shattering approach to its historical subjects and placed them in relation to fictional characters, *Mrs. Parker* takes a more straightforward biographical approach. Rudolph and his cast and crew have shown an attention to detail in recapturing a sense of the period, and much of what is depicted in the film is historically accurate (at least if the biographers of the period and the writings of the participants themselves are to be believed). Yet, like *The Moderns,* Rudolph demonstrates that these characters were in the process of creating their own myths of themselves. Anticipating the performance-art concept of later decades, the members of the Algonquin Round Table found their most lasting creations to be their own images. As one character comments late in the film, they became famous mainly for having lunch. If *The Moderns* takes place at a time when art is giving way to commercialism, *Mrs. Parker and the Vicious Circle* demonstrates the birth of the cult of celebrity. *The Moderns* depicts a disparity between artistic pursuit and representatives of commerce who seek to determine what constitutes art. The protagonists in *Mrs. Parker* exist in both worlds, pursuing their literary endeavors while earning money as columnists and critics who influence public perception of the work of others. As Rudolph demonstrates, however, the attempts of the members of the vicious circle to perpetuate their public image conflict with their personal artistic pursuits, and the group becomes a detriment to individual expression. The concept is expressed early in the film, when Parker observes that the table produced "no real greats, just a lot of loudmouths showing off"—a comment that will be reinforced by a psychoanalyst's examination of the group dynamic late in the film.

As in many of Rudolph's films, the focus is on triangular configurations within this larger group. The main emphasis is on the relationship between Dorothy Parker (Jennifer Jason Leigh) and Robert Benchley (Campbell Scott), which remains unrequited because of Benchley's family obligations and Parker's series of unsatisfactory relationships. Parker recalls other Rudolph heroines in her desire to find a perfect relationship while maintaining her own individuality and unknown qualities.

Comparison to *Welcome to L.A.* is invited by the opening shots of Parker removing a cigarette from a circular holder and bringing it to her lips as she begins to recite the poem, "Into love and out again / Thus I went and thus I go." Although, like Karen, she addresses the camera, making the audience a conspirator in her discourse on love, Rudolph presents this opening shot in fragmented images, indicating the enigmatic nature of the heroine. Rudolph emphasizes the importance of language as he stays on her lips while she recites, and then tilts up to show her eyes as the poem ends, indicating a degree of mystery to Parker that even her own words cannot penetrate.

This opening shot is presented in black and white, and the mono-chrome carries over to a shot of Benchley filming one of his cele-brated shorts on a Hollywood soundstage (the shot matted to con-form to the proper aspect ratio of the original film). At the conclusion of the take, the camera follows Benchley as he walks out of the matted frame and into the widescreen composition. After taking a book con-taining liquor from an assistant ("The top one's a corker"), Benchley exits and encounters Parker and her husband, Alan Campbell (Peter Gallagher), outside. In an establishment of her character, Parker's first line in the film proper is an obscenity. Rudolph frames the characters in a three-shot, establishing the film's key visual motif, with the unre-quited relationship of Parker and Benchley continually undermined by the presence of another character. Campbell leaves, and Rudolph stays on an extended two-shot of Benchley and Parker while they dis-cuss her efforts to form a writers' union (Benchley joking that she sent him a note in red ink), their body language suggesting an addi-tional level of communication beyond the words they are exchanging. Their momentary reunion is interrupted by a production assistant, and Parker comments, "Visiting hours are over, Mr. Benchley," imply-ing a comparison between Hollywood (or at least the studio system) and prison. As he accompanies her to the soundstage, the assistant comments that things must have been so colorful in the 1920s, setting up the full color flashback to follow.

This opening scene (with an extended camera track that recalls Robert Altman's *The Player* [1992]) establishes the main romantic conflict in the movie, as well as the contrast between the bleak lives the principals experienced in Hollywood and the more exuberant existence in the New York of the 1920s, which will make up the majority of the film. The transformation to the earlier decade is accomplished through a visual pun, as the director on the soundstage yells "Cut," and the film literally cuts to the 1920s with a shot of a pair of scissors trimming an article from a newspaper, presented in color and supported by Mark Isham's swing jazz score. The reference to a more colorful past, while reinforced visually, implies that the flashbacks are filtered through memory and represent a myth of the era that the participants helped to foster. Like the stylized flashback scenes in *Equinox* or the recollection in *Mortal Thoughts,* the past in *Mrs. Parker* is filtered through an individual's perception.

The flashback begins when Parker, Benchley, and Robert Sherwood (Nick Cassavetes) are working for *Vanity Fair.* Theater critic Parker is berated by editor Frank Crowninshield (played by Robert Benchley's grandson Peter Benchley) for attacking a play produced by a major advertiser. Although her male co-workers sympathize with her, the scene establishes her position in a male-dominated society and reinforces the notion of individual expression coming in conflict with commercial gain. Later, with Parker alone in her apartment, Rudolph provides a quick shot of a piece of paper in her typewriter on which she has written the single line, "Please, God, let me write like a man." Of course, Parker's great contribution to literature was that she helped to redefine writing by women. The typed sentence, however, indicates the perception, against which she rebeled, that writing by women at the time could only be associated with certain feminine (rather than feminist) concerns. Throughout the film, Parker will make references to the superficial nature of her writing and her objection that she continues to write about "brokenhearted sissies." Parker's private reverie concludes with a characteristic Rudolph mirror shot, once again establishing the concept of identity and equating that identity with a denial of the feminine.

Parker is interrupted by the return of her soldier husband, Eddie (Andrew McCarthy), and the implication that he is a part of her identity is made by a shot of him in a mirror as she pours him a drink. She joins him in the mirrored reflection as the two of them fall onto the couch, but Rudolph cuts to the "real" shot as she pulls away, and Eddie asks, "Don't you want to feel married again." The cut establishes a contrast between the reflected image of marital bliss and the reality, in which outside forces are pulling the two apart. Parker rejects his embrace because she has to be at the theater in a half hour to review a play, and although she tries to get Eddie to accompany her, she ends up sitting with Benchley. When she returns to the apartment, she panics at the sight of Eddie's hypodermic needle and runs into the bedroom to wake him. The scene is followed by a monochromatic shot of Parker reciting "The Lady's Reward," addressing the deceptions women are expected to enact to maintain a relationship and the belief that it is not worth the compromise.

The first of the triangular relationships, involving Parker, Benchley, and Eddie, becomes the focus of the next section, with the situation complicated by Parker's professional difficulties. A second triangular configuration is created by Benchley's marriage to Gertrude (Jennifer Beals). Gertrude answers the phone when Parker calls their suburban home on a Sunday to tell Benchley she has been fired. As Benchley talks to Parker on the phone, Rudolph frames Gertrude on the opposite side of a wall partition, indicating the separation between husband and wife. Later Benchley consoles Parker at her apartment, and the two are seated in the foreground as Eddie dances alone in the background.

In the film, Parker's dismissal from *Vanity Fair* becomes equated with the creation of the Algonquin Round Table (though in actuality the group grew out of a luncheon meeting arranged by John Peter Toohey, a press agent for Eugene O'Neil, to get back at Alexander Woolcott). Rudolph presents the inauguration of the "vicious circle" as a scene reminiscent of the stateroom scene in *A Night at the Opera* (1935), with Parker, Benchley, and Sherwood going to lunch at the hotel and being joined in their tiny booth by more and more members of the literary and journalistic set. The sense of immediate camaraderie is offset by the implication that the group is intruding on a private moment, setting a pattern for the conflict throughout the

The Round Table holds court in *Mrs. Parker and the Vicious Circle* (1994), with Parker (Jennifer Jason Leigh) at the upper center and Robert Benchley (Campbell Scott) seated on her right. Throughout *Mrs. Parker and the Vicious Circle* Rudolph contrasts the circularity of the Round Table with the triangular nature of Parker's relationships.
Courtesy Museum of Modern Art/Film Stills Archive.

film on the compulsive need to be together and the manner in which this interferes with the personal lives of the group's members.

Throughout the scene, between the various bon mots, Benchley has been trying to make a speech about his decision to resign from the magazine in sympathy with Parker. When he finally succeeds in making the proclamation, Parker abruptly leaves the table. Benchley follows, and the two retreat to a private corner of the hotel lobby, where (in another of Rudolph's lengthy single takes) they discuss the notion of getting an office together. Indicating the unresolved nature of their relationship, Parker comments, "I feel as though you're proposing marriage," and Benchley responds, "How many torments lie in the small circle of a wedding ring." Parker tells him she could kiss him but it might not come out right, and she expresses the fear that she might lose him. This moment defines their association, with Parker indicating that it will remain unfulfilled because of her fear that consummating their relationship might end it.

The scenes of Parker and Benchley setting up their office are accompanied by Parker's recitation of the poem "Daydreams." The idyllic quality of the opening lines ("We'd build a little bungalow / If you and I were one"), associated visually with her relationship with Benchley, are contrasted with the sharper edge of the final couplet ("And so I think it best, my love, / To string along as two"), equated on screen with Parker and Eddie moving into a new apartment. As if to emphasize that this moment is an inversion of the truth of their marriage, Rudolph again shows Parker and Eddie reflected in a mirror as they meet their new neighbor, artist Neysa McMein (Rebecca Miller).

The seemingly euphoric mood continues in a montage depicting Horatio Byrd (Wallace Shawn), head waiter at the Algonquin, coming up with the notion of the round table and carrying it through. In both *The Moderns* and *Mrs. Parker,* his two films that make most extensive use of long takes, Rudolph incorporates a montage depicting the act of creation, as though editing itself was regarded as an aspect of the creative process. The Algonquin montage ends on a high-angle shot of the full group, and the camera moves in to a close-up of Parker laughing, in one of her only moments of genuine joy in the film. The party atmosphere carries over to her private life, with her apartment house providing a second gathering place for the group.

At one such party, the triangular configurations converge, as the Benchleys encounter the Parkers kissing in a corner of the room. Rudolph narrows the group shot to alternating close-ups of the two women, then pulls out, as Eddie leaves, to present a three-shot of

Parker and the Benchleys, while the other members of the circle watch from the sidelines and comment on Benchley and his two wives. Soon after, Parker goes in search of Eddie and finds him in the bathroom, where a still has been set up. Eddie has become upset because of the cutting remarks Parker has made about him to her friends and lashes out at her, then immediately tries to comfort her. As he leaves, Parker seeks solace in alcohol, and Rudolph continues the extended take by panning across the room to reveal Gertrude hiding in a stall, from which she has witnessed the encounter. The women exchange awkward glances, and Gertrude expresses her gratitude that Benchley does not drink. She asks Parker if she likes alcohol, and Parker responds, "Not much, but it's better than a sock in the eye" (recalling the closing lines of her poem "Inventory": "Three be the things I shall have till I die: / Laughter and hope and a sock in the eye").

The alcoholism, which is already becoming a means for Parker to escape from her troubled personal and professional experiences, will also shortly affect Benchley. During a review produced by the members of the Round Table, Benchley and Parker share a moment backstage in which he expresses disdain over her drinking habits. She suggests the motivation for her increasing alcoholism when she indicates that Eddie has left her to return to Hartford. Following his successful presentation of "The Treasurer's Report," Benchley and the others go to Tony Soma's speakeasy to celebrate, and, despite his professed aversion to liquor, Benchley takes his first drink. This seemingly innocent gesture will have a profound impact on the humorist, as he becomes an alcoholic and abandons the domesticity of his life with Gertrude.

The review that becomes the source of Benchley's deterioration provides renewed hope for Parker. Backstage at the production, Woolcott (Tom McGowan) introduces his newest discovery, Chicago journalist Charles MacArthur (Matthew Broderick). Although Parker greets him with a typically cutting comment, by the end of the review an undeniable attraction has developed between them. Rudolph emphasizes the shifting dynamic to a new triangular relationship in a backstage shot in which Gertrude and members of the company frame Parker and MacArthur in the background. Rudolph slowly tightens in on the couple as Benchley joins them to announce the news that he has been hired to perform "The Treasurer's Report" as part of a legitimate review. Gertrude is defocused in the foreground during this exchange. Benchley moves forward to her, and the two move out of frame, while the camera stays on Parker and MacArthur as she asks if he wants a drink before kissing her.

During the postperformance celebration, Rudolph emphasizes the intimacy of Parker and MacArthur within the larger group dynamic. MacArthur observes that Parker probably has more fun drinking with them than she did with Eddie because she was married to him, and adds that it also might be more fun sleeping with someone else. Parker is presented in a tight close-up as she warns that the subject is in danger of turning to sex, and then alternating close-ups of MacArthur and Benchley are presented while she observes that an experienced woman is in a position to tell how the other fellow does it, but that it would be bad manners to do so.

Parker, Benchley, and MacArthur leave the speakeasy together and, while MacArthur sneaks back to get their personal belongings, Parker indicates to Benchley that she is falling in love with the young journalist. Rudolph provides the lengthiest single take in the film, as the trio takes refuge from the rain in MacArthur's apartment. The scene begins with a three-shot of Benchley sitting and MacArthur and Parker standing, then pans to become a two-shot of MacArthur and Parker. When MacArthur suggests that he has read more about her than by her, implying that she is known more for her image than her actual work, she moves away from him to a two-shot with Benchley. MacArthur pulls her back and begins to talk about a story she has written, which he assumes is based on Benchley. The exchange ends as they enter the bedroom. As the couple falls onto the bed, leaving the door partially open, Benchley comes into the frame momentarily and then discretely exits.

An intimate exchange between MacArthur and Parker in bed, again presented in a single take, is followed by their announcement to the group of their engagement, and another party scene to celebrate. Once again, the group is presented in conflict with personal relationships, as MacArthur is shown standing over Parker while he holds court with the other members of the circle. The group's insensitivity to the problems of its own members is suggested as the men, while playing poker, discuss Parker's apparent melancholia and one observes, "Dotty can't be suffering and still say all those funny things."

The extent of Parker's suffering becomes apparent in the next scenes, as she discovers she is pregnant, and also arrives at MacArthur's apartment unannounced to find that he has been sleeping with an actress. Parker has an abortion, and once again she seeks comfort in the group and in alcohol. During their binge she describes a postabortion nightmare in which she sees God hovering over her but cannot understand what he is saying because he is wearing a surgical mask. Her apparent guilt over the abortion, combined with her chronic depression, alcoholism, and the end of her relationship with MacArthur, culminates in a suicide attempt. Rudolph presents this as a spontaneous gesture, as Parker finds a razor while angrily tossing out the contents of her medicine cabinet. Indicating the shattering of her sense of identity, Rudolph shows Parker's reflection in the mirrored door of the cabinet before she picks up the razor, then zooms into her eyes and down to her hands as she picks it up and opens it, and then returns to a medium close-up of her face. As she slashes her wrists (an action presented out of the range of the camera), Rudolph pans back to her reflection in the mirror. Following the suicide attempt, Parker is shown in another of the black-and-white recitation scenes, presenting the brief and bitter poem "Two-Volume Novel," the last line of which ("He didn't love back") describes all of her relationships up to this point and could refer to Eddie, Benchley, or MacArthur.

The suicide attempt becomes a turning point for Parker. As if to demonstrate her attempt to reestablish her identity, Rudolph follows a scene of her being visited in the hospital by the members of the group with a shot of her portrait being painted by McMein, although a brief close-up of her clenched hands indicates that all is not well. Parker responds to her failed relationships and her self-destructive tendencies by entering into a series of frivolous encounters, while at the same time trying to come to terms with her desires. During another speakeasy visit with Benchley, she expresses her wish to "go wild" and also questions why the two of them never consummated their relationship. The more reserved Benchley pulls away from her and expresses a kind of mock-indignation at the question. Parker concludes, "The things I want the most I can't seem to get." Instead, she amuses herself by inviting a woman at the speakeasy to join them and introduces Benchley as a talent scout. Her frivolous encounters continue at one of Woolcott's elaborate lawn parties. After bringing the activity to a grinding halt with a withering recitation of "Résumé" (itemizing the inefficiency of various forms of suicide) when she is asked to entertain, she sneaks off into the bushes with a dullish guest for a short-lived liaison.

Parker takes a room in the Algonquin and, under pressure to pay the rent, writes a play. It is unsuccessful (even though her colleagues point out that it got good reviews, and some of them were even from strangers), and the impression is again given that it was about Benchley. Parker retreats to the comfort of the group after the play, and the table for once grows silent when Benchley arrives. After the others depart, Rudolph presents a shot reminiscent of the concluding scene of the breakfast table montage in *Citizen Kane* (1941), showing Parker and Benchley seated at opposite ends of the great table (in contrast to the intimacy of the scene following formation of the group, in which Parker and Benchley shared a crowded office), indicating the distance that has grown between them, as well as the alienation they feel when not surrounded by the rest of the circle. Another opportunity is provided to consummate their relationship when Parker faints while visiting the whorehouse where Benchley has taken up residence. Benchley carries her upstairs to one of the bedrooms and the camera tightens in on the two of them in bed, but then follows Benchley as he gets up to leave.

This unresolved encounter is paralleled a short time later, when Parker meets Eddie on the street. After he buys her a dog, she invites him to lunch, but he indicates that he is meeting someone. Parker puts on a mask by pretending she also has a date, but after they part the camera follows her in a lengthy tracking shot as she wanders the street alone with her new canine companion. During this scene, Parker provides a voice-over recitation of "Symptom Recital," which concludes, "I'm due to fall in love again." Fulfilling this prophecy, she returns to the hotel to find Deems Taylor (James LeGros) waiting for her. In a composition that echoes her earlier encounter with MacArthur, the two of them are shown in a two-shot as they fall onto the bed.

Parker's series of meaningless encounters ends with a flashforward to the Hollywood of the 1940s, where her marriage to Alan Campbell is crumbling. While talking to her colleagues in the writers' building, one of them brings in the news that Benchley has died, a victim of his alcoholism. Parker retreats to her office and sits at her desk. Suddenly she smashes a bottle and them breaks down in mourning for "Dear Fred" (the private nickname she had for Benchley). Rudolph stays on her back as she turns to the window, her body language indicating her extreme grief, then cuts to an exterior view of her framed in her office window, followed by a jump cut to a wider shot that emphasizes her emotional alienation.

The inclination might have been to end the film with Benchley's death, but by placing this scene where he does, Rudolph is able to bring an added dimension to the final flashback of a scene with the full group. The occasion is a New Year's Eve party, and there is a sense throughout the scene that the group is disintegrating. The casual affair with Deems Taylor is briefly alluded to in a three-shot of Parker, Taylor, and his wife, Mary Kennedy (Heather Graham). Parker also encounters MacArthur at the party, and he comments on her passion for unhappiness as the two exchange cold, emotionless stares. She has a potential moment of privacy with Benchley, but it is interrupted when he is dragged away by another party guest.

Also attending the affair is a Freudian psychoanalyst ("I'm afreud of that man," one of the guests quips), and he finds a willing subject in Parker. The two close themselves off in a room while the party continues around them, and Parker acknowledges her despair and frustration. The analyst tells her, "It's not what you're suffering, Mrs. Parker, it's what you're missing." He extends his observation to the group as a whole, and comments that their constant compulsion to be with each other is a sign of insecurity. He also suggests that this compulsion is preventing the members of the group from realizing their individual potential as writers and artists. Rudolph cuts from their party conversation to the analyst's office (where he keeps a variety of masks and cultural artifacts, as well as a statue of a headless and armless Venus, which in itself is open to a range of Freudian interpretations), as Parker continues her self-exploration. The camera shares her introspection as it slowly dollies in while she analyzes herself, and she concludes by telling the therapist that her version of pain is more fun than his. As she leaves, George S. Kaufman (David Thornton) enters and insecurely asks if she said anything about him, indicating that the entire group will quite likely find themselves in the doctor's chambers.

Painful as her realization is, Parker's acceptance of her depressive state becomes a form of independence, and the final scenes find her alone with her private recollections of the past, which are at odds with the image she helped to create. These scenes take place in New York in 1958 (again presented in black and white). As Parker sits in a bar (with the television showing A Star Is Born [1937], for which she and Alan Campbell wrote the script), she is approached by an actor named Fred (Stanley Tucci) and two female companions. Fred (who commented to his companions when they first saw Parker sitting alone that she was mainly famous for having lunch) indicates that he worked on a film she scripted, for which the director was blacklisted, and tries to talk to her about her experiences in Hollywood. Parker harasses him for bringing up the past, and as he and his companions depart, she begins to reminisce about the other "Fred" she once loved.

Jennifer Jason Leigh as Dorothy Parker. Despite her involvement in the famous Algonquin Round Table, Parker is often depicted as an isolated and melancholy figure.
Courtesy Museum of Modern Art/Film Stills Archive.

The film concludes with Parker being honored with an award and surprising the assemblage with an abrupt acceptance speech in which she comments, "I never thought I'd make it," and then departs. As she exits down an expressionistically lit stairway, a brief written statement describes her death. Rudolph presents the cast credits over a 360-degree shot of the members of the Round Table, which ends on a shot of Parker and Benchley, then zooms to a close-up of the heroine. The remainder of the credits are presented over shots of the elderly Parker being interviewed by reporters, in which she briefly alludes to her political views and defends the writers who came out of her generation—a statement that contradicts her observation at the start of the film that the group produced no real giants.

Aside from the early references to unionizing, a brief allusion to the blacklist during her conversation with the actor in 1958 and the questions by reporters about Parker's involvement in the Spanish Civil War, little is made of the heroine's political beliefs. Instead, in keeping with the direction of his past work, Rudolph focuses on Parker's attempts to find romantic fulfillment and her frustration at never being able to reconcile the one great love of her life. Her relationship with Benchley takes on attributes of the comedies of remarriage, particularly in their shared language and pet names for each other, but her fear that she will lose the relationship by fulfilling it ultimately leaves Parker alone and with a part of herself unknown to him. While her periodic address to the camera would seem to equate Parker with Karen in *Welcome to L.A.*, she actually begins to parallel Carroll in her attempt to find her own identity in a series of encounters, although there is a greater sense of emotional commitment in her affairs, at least with Eddie, MacArthur, and Benchley (the relationship with Alan Campbell, whom she married twice, is not developed to any great degree in the film), and it is her feelings of loss that make her a more tragic figure.

While the larger group in *Welcome to L.A.* was chiefly a structure out of which the various triangular configurations developed, in *Mrs. Parker and the Vicious Circle* it becomes a source of relationships, both instigating and undermining them. Throughout the film there is a geometric conflict between triangularity and circularity, with Parker retreating to the circle whenever one of her relationships ends. Yet as the film's full title implies, the group itself is hardly a form of comfort. Despite their mutual dependency, the members continually stab one another in the back (with the one who is being dissected often showing up just as the conversation about him or her ends). If anything, Rudolph and co-writer Randy Sue Coburn's treatment of this aspect of the film is too polite, and the self-named vicious circle does not come across as anywhere near as competitive as it undoubtedly was.

This may in part be due to Rudolph's framing of the scenes involving the group as a memory that has been clouded by the "colorful" image the Round Table has achieved. The conflict between image and truth is characteristic of Rudolph's entire output. Although he does not indulge in the kind of direct defiance of convention that has occurred in many of his other works, the director provides a few incidents that call into question our perception of reality. The first shot of Benchley moving from the matted frame of his short film to the widescreen image is momentarily disorienting, and Rudolph later provides a shot backstage at the review in which Benchley walks through a door, which is then carried away and proves to have been a prop. Even more reflective of Rudolph's other work is a brief dream sequence in which, in a single take, Benchley is shown in Parker's apartment and, as he moves to the bedroom, is replaced by MacArthur, who kneels beside Parker on the bed, after which the camera pulls back to reveal her waking up alone. Whereas past Rudolph films had characters sharing dreams, here the director varies the formula by having a dream share characters.

On a more general level, *Mrs. Parker* reinforces the notion of deception that has carried through Rudolph's work. Parker and Eddie, as well as the Benchleys, maintain a facade of happy domesticity despite the tensions that are affecting their personal relationships. When MacArthur first meets Parker he tells her she is his favorite writer but later admits he is not very familiar with her work. She responds by telling him, "I lied when I smiled."

The concept of deception, of course, carries over to the depiction of the group as a whole and ties in to the contrast between public image and private reality. Early in the film, when Kaufman is acknowledged as a celebrity, he dismisses the comment by saying he is only a temporary one, and a colleague responds that there is no other kind. Nevertheless, the Round Table members established the notion of permanent celebrity and succeeded in securing their immortality by contributing to the creation of their own image. The endless flow of witticisms and attempts to top one another disguised their own insecurities, and Dorothy Parker's position at the center of the circle (the life of the party) masked her own loneliness and depression. These aspects of her character surfaced not in her public image and in her quoted conversations but in the often bitter and poignant works she left behind. Rudolph's incorporation of the monochromatic shots of Parker reciting her work enable the viewer to get beyond deception and image and get at the emotional reality he strives to find in all of his characters.

While the image of the Algonquin Round Table is one of urbane wit and humor, Rudolph uses the subject to present one of his darkest visions. Working with a historical figure, Rudolph is unable to offer the potential redemption afforded to characters in even his bleakest previous works. Even Henry, posed at the brink of the Grand Canyon in *Equinox,* has a choice of jumping or starting over. Parker is given no such epiphany and can only offer the world-weary declaration of independence, stated in one of her poems, that "I will stay the way I am / Because I do not give a damn." In *Mrs. Parker and the Vicious Circle,* the heroine is not a victim of synthetic emotion but of real emotions that cannot be reconciled and from which there is no escape.

CONCLUSION

Mrs. Parker and the Vicious Circle at once provides a summation of Rudolph's work up to this point and offers evidence of a new direction. The film might be regarded as signalling a new realism in the director's work, particularly in the attention to detail in capturing its period and characters. A Bazanian theorist might also suggest that Rudolph's prominent use of long takes reinforces this move toward greater realism. But as the director has pointed out on many occasions, reality is deceptive. The necessity of re-creating in detail a time and place that no longer exist (once again using Montreal as a stand-in for the actual locations) in itself verifies the director's contention that film is a lie on reality. Rudolph's most recent director-for-hire project, *Mortal Thoughts,* also suggests a level of realism in its attention to the everyday details in the lives of its Bayonne, New Jersey, residents, but this is at the service of a narrative that, more than any of Rudolph's previous work, calls into question our ability to determine truth.

Whether or not *Mrs. Parker* anticipates a new direction in Rudolph's work, it serves to reconcile the two phases of his directorial career, placing his personal concerns and visual style within a more conventional narrative framework, while once again reinforcing both his connection to and his deviations from Robert Altman. Most directors who have been recognized as having a personal vision have developed it either within the studio system or independent of it, but Rudolph continues to work in both capacities. Although many of his more widely touted contemporaries, such as David Lynch, have begun to show evidence that they are more visual than visionary, Rudolph's recent films indicate that he has found ways to develop and refine his vision even within projects that he regards as less personal.

While Rudolph's work continues to defy established notions of narrative structure and suggests new possibilities for the medium, it also challenges accepted modes of production. Working with limited budgets and tight shooting schedules, Rudolph has been able to create films that are even more successful at depicting a unique world than many big-budget works. *Choose Me,* for example, stands as proof that a quality product can be achieved for under $1 million. Like Altman, Rudolph has developed a reputation as an actor's director, which allows him to attract name performers for a good deal less than they would be paid for a studio project. Rudolph's films offer a challenge to the Hollywood system in which he grew up and that has become characterized by excess.

In Rudolph's worldview such excess has become equated with an alienation of emotions. Audiences have been trained in an almost Pavlovian way to respond to the manufactured emotions and predictability of much of mainstream filmmaking. Rudolph's defiance of accepted conventions forces viewers to make connections with his films rather than remain passive observers. As such, their emotional stake in the lives and pursuits of the characters becomes much higher, even as the characters themselves seek to get in touch with their emotions in an environment that increasingly discourages such contact.

As Rudolph's work has developed, this connection between an alienating society and the effect it has on individuals has become more pronounced. In less personal films, such as *Roadie* and *Songwriter,* the manufacturing of image and marketing of emotions is treated in a largely comic way, and his central characters remain individualists who are able to overcome the threat of commercialization. In *Choose Me* the protagonists are ultimately able to get beyond the processed romanticism on which they are initially dependent, including Dr. Love herself, who tells a caller near the end of the film that she needs to be careful not to listen to her own advice. Even when working in darker tones, such as the environments depicted in *Trouble in Mind* and *Equinox,* Rudolph has offered his characters an opportunity to develop a stronger sense of themselves.

With more recent works, the threat to human emotions has become greater and more dangerous. Yet as his vision of urban decay and moral disintegration has become more pronounced, Rudolph's films have also taken on a more spiritual dimension. The search for self has become equated with a search for a spiritual awareness that can only be achieved by escaping from what Rudolph calls "the Big Lie" of materialism.

Whether exposing the myth of Buffalo Bill or Paris in the 1920s, Rudolph indicates that much of what we take for reality is a deception. Like Henry at the end of *Equinox,* he suggests it is only by discovering the lie of our existence that we can begin to recognize its truth. Rudolph has continually pointed out in interviews that people have accused his films of being strange but that they are actually much closer to the absurdity of what we call real life than more conventionally constructed products. In a world increasingly characterized by depersonalization and deception, he offers hope that people can still connect.

As of this writing, Rudolph has no specific projects in preparation. For some time he has talked about making a live-action version of his friend Gary Larson's newspaper comic *The Far Side,* but Rudolph's frequent producer David Blocker indicated recently that the project does not appear likely to happen anytime soon. The film, if produced, might bring Rudolph to the attention of a much wider audience. Another long-standing project, the film version of Kurt Vonnegut's *Breakfast of Champions,* for which Rudolph wrote the script during his initial association with Robert Altman, is also being discussed for future production, as is a film of Tom Robbins's novel *Skinny Legs and All.* Both projects would signal another new direction for Rudolph's work, as he has never adapted a literary source to film, and it will be interesting to see how his personal vision combines with those of established writers. Still another possible project, a biography of Man Ray, sounds more in keeping with the director's recent work and would once again allow him to deal with issues of art and reality.

Rudolph himself is optimistic about the future direction of his career. "I'm very excited about these changes in my work," he has stated. "I feel like I have to surrender to what's happening to me. I don't know what that is. It's like the tide on the move. . . . Suddenly tomorrow will be different, and I'm always eager about that" (Brooks, 62).

NOTES AND REFERENCES

Preface

1. Rex Reed, *New York Post,* 1 November 1984, 34.
2. Stephen Farber, "Five Horsemen after the Apocalypse," *Film Comment,* July–August 1985, 34; hereafter cited in text.
3. Stanley Cavell, "Psychoanalysis and Cinema: The Melodrama of the Unknown Woman," in *Images in Our Souls* (Baltimore: Johns Hopkins University Press, 1987), 18; hereafter cited in text.

Introduction: Defining the Rudolph Universe

1. David Rensin, "The Man Who Would Be Different," *American Film,* March 1986, 53; hereafter cited in text.
2. Gavin Smith, "Alan Rudolph: I Don't Have a Career, I Have a Careen," *Film Comment,* May–June 1993, 60; hereafter cited in text.
3. A. Garel and F. Guérif, "Notes sur Alan Rudolph; Entretien avec Alan Rudolph," *Revue du Cinéma,* July–August 1985, 80; hereafter cited in text.
4. "Add Romance and a Crazed World," *Monthly Film Bulletin,* August 1985, 264; hereafter cited in text.
5. Richard Combs, "Joyce and Fitzgerald Never Robbed a Bank," *Monthly Film Bulletin,* March 1989, 69; hereafter cited in text.

Chapter 1

1. Another film of the period with a science fiction element and presented from a child's point of view, William Cameron Menzies's *Invaders from Mars* (1953), has been acknowledged by Rudolph as one of his early influences.
2. F. Anthony Macklin, "Welcome to Lion's Gate: Interviews with Director Alan Rudolph and Composer Richard Baskin," *Film Heritage,* Fall 1976, 2; hereafter cited in text.
3. F. Anthony Macklin, *"Buffalo Bill and the Indians,"* *Film Heritage,* Fall 1976, 39.
4. "Disneyland by Night," *Film Comment,* January–February 1977, 13; hereafter cited in text.

Chapter 3

1. Tom Milne, "As Suggestive as a Neon Orchid," *Sight and Sound,* Summer 1985, 215; hereafter cited in text.

Chapter 4

1. Rudolph has indicated that this was the one scene in the film he covered in detail and that the version in the film was actually the rehearsal, which he decided to use only when he was preparing to edit the footage (Smith, 61).

Chapter 6

1. Karen Jaehne, "Time for *The Moderns,*" *Film Comment,* April 1988, 28; hereafter cited in text.
2. Eva Rueschmann, "Desire and Loss in Alan Rudolph's *The Moderns,*" *Literature/Film Quarterly* 22, no. 1 (1994): 59.
3. Richard Trainor, "*The Moderns,*" *Sight and Sound,* Autumn 1988, 233; hereafter cited in text.

Chapter 7

1. Philip Strick, "*Love at Large,*" *Monthly Film Bulletin,* November 1990, 328.

Chapter 8

1. Rosetta Brooks, "Soul City: Rosetta Brooks Talks with Alan Rudolph," *Artforum,* January 1993, 61; hereafter cited in text.

Chapter 9

1. Philip Strick, "*The Impure,*" *Monthly Film Bulletin,* January 1989, 31.

SELECTED BIBLIOGRAPHY

Primary Works

"Add Romance and a Crazed World." *Monthly Film Bulletin,* August 1985, 264. Rudolph responds to written questions about his work with Altman and his films up through *Choose Me.*

Buffalo Bill and the Indians, or Sitting Bull's History Lesson. With Robert Altman. New York: Bantam Books, 1976. Published screenplay for the film directed by Altman.

"Disneyland by Night." *Film Comment,* January–February 1977, 10–13. Rudolph writes about his background, his association with Altman, and the making of *Welcome to L.A.*

Movies for a Desert Island, edited by Ellen Oumano, 154–59. New York: St. Martin's Press, 1987. Chapter on Rudolph gives background on his career and discusses films that influenced him, including *Invaders from Mars* (1953), *Stagecoach* (1939), and *How Green Was My Valley* (1941). He also expresses his admiration for Altman, Stanley Kubrick, and Walter Hill.

Secondary Works

Books and Parts of Books

Cavell, Stanley. "Psychoanalysis and Cinema: The Melodrama of the Unknown Woman." In *Images in Our Souls,* edited by Joseph H. Smith and William Kerrigan, 11–43. Baltimore: John Hopkins University Press, 1987. Cavell outlines the basic criteria for his genre of the melodrama of the unknown woman. Although he does not make reference to Rudolph's work, several of his concepts have been applied in this evaluation of the director's work.

———. "Psychoanalysis and Cinema: The Melodrama of the Unknown Woman." In *Trial(s) of Psychoanalysis,* edited by Francoise Meltzer, 227–58. Chicago: University of Chicago Press, 1988. Revision of preceding article.

———. *Pursuits of Happiness.* Cambridge, Mass.: Harvard University Press, 1981. Outlines the criteria for what Cavell has defined as the comedy of remarriage and analyzes it in relation to several films. Although Cavell does not deal with Rudolph's work, a number of his concepts have been applied to the analysis of the director's films in this text.

148

Coburn, Randy Sue. *Trouble in Mind*. Los Angeles: Alive Press, 1986. Novel-
ization of the screenplay by Rudolph.

McNab, G. C. *International Dictionary of Films and Filmmakers*, vol. 2, 2d ed.,
edited by Nicholas Thomas. Chicago: St. James Press, 1991. The entry on
Rudolph provides a brief assessment of his career, with an undertone of
elitist negativity, suggesting that despite the director's relegation to the
art houses he is a populist filmmaker.

Maltin, Leonard, ed. *Leonard Maltin's Movie Encyclopedia*. New York: Dutton,
1994. Provides a brief overview of the director's career, with few critical
observations.

Thomson, David. *A Biographical Dictionary of Film*, 3d ed. New York: Alfred A.
Knopf, 1994. As with the Maltin encyclopedia, this volume contains a
brief entry on Rudolph that provides an overview of his career.

Wilson, David. "Robert Altman." In *Close-Up: The Contemporary Director*,
edited by Jon Tuska, 153–205. Metuchen, N.J.: Scarecrow Press, 1981.
The chapter on Altman was written as the director was involved in producing *Welcome to L.A.* Wilson visited the set of the Rudolph film, and
the article contains observations and comments from Rudolph, Sissy
Spacek, and Keith Carradine. The article gives very early insight into
Rudolph's working methods and his admiration for Altman.

Journal Articles

Baxter, Brian. "Happy with Trouble." *Films and Filming*, September 1986,
26–27. Brief interview with the director at the time of the release of
Trouble in Mind.

Brooks, Rosetta. "Soul City: Rosetta Brooks Talks with Alan Rudolph." *Artforum*, January 1993, 56–62. Interview with the director that opens with
discussion of *Choose Me* and covers Rudolph's work up through
Equinox, with particular emphasis on *Choose Me, The Moderns*, and
Equinox.

Combs, Richard. "Joyce and Fitzgerald Never Robbed a Bank." *Monthly Film
Bulletin*, March 1989, 67–69. Interview with Rudolph about the making of *The Moderns* and his ideas about art, deception, and the Paris of
the 1920s. Presented as an adjunct to Tom Milne's review of the film.

Farber, Stephen. "Five Horsemen after the Apocalypse." *Film Comment*,
July–August 1985, 32–35. The article focuses on five directors considered mavericks who work outside the Hollywood system. In addition to
comments from Rudolph, it includes observations from producer Carolyn Pfeiffer.

Garel, A., and F. Guérif. "Notes sur Alan Rudolph; Entretien avec Alan
Rudolph." *Revue du Cinéma*, July–August 1985, 76–85. Provides back-
ground on the director and an interview covering his work up through
Trouble in Mind. Although the questions are rather basic, Rudolph pro-

vides some insight into his work and on the problems encountered in his studio-generated productions. Includes a filmography and biographical information. The article was specially translated for this book by Joy Macy.

Gravett, Sharon. " 'Boats against the Current': The Presence of the Past in *The Moderns.*" *Post Script,* Winter–Spring 1994, 28–34. Discusses the difficulty in distinguishing between appearance and reality in *The Moderns* and draws comparisons between the film and literature of the period, particularly *The Great Gatsby.*

Jaehne, Karen. "Time for *The Moderns.*" *Film Comment,* April 1988, 24–29. A discussion of the film with comments and interpretation by the director. Also deals with the director's other work and includes comments from Keith Carradine.

Macklin, F. Anthony. "Welcome to Lion's Gate: Interviews with Director Alan Rudolph and Composer Richard Baskin." *Film Heritage,* Fall 1976, 1–17. Contains interviews with the director and composer at the time of the release of *Welcome to L.A.* Particularly helpful for its information on Altman's Lion's Gate studio and for Rudolph's comments on his association with Altman. Also gives some insight into Rudolph's integration of music and film.

Milne, Tom. "As Suggestive as a Neon Orchid." *Sight and Sound,* Summer 1985, 214–16. Milne discusses *Choose Me* in relation to *Welcome to L.A.* and *Remember My Name.* He is critical of *Welcome to L.A.* but praises the other two films and suggests that they establish a true auteurist's vision.

Murphy, Kathleen. "Only Angels Have Wings." *Film Comment.* July–August 1991, 26–29. Discusses *Mortal Thoughts* in relation to *Thelma and Louise,* as films dealing with "wild girls of the road" that contradict the gender orientation of American road fiction. Also draws some parallels between Rudolph's film and Hitchcock's *Marnie* (1964).

Rensin, David. "The Man Who Would Be Different." *American Film,* March 1986, 50–54. Discusses the director's work up through *Trouble in Mind* and divides it into personal and studio projects. Includes comments from Genevieve Bujold, Keith Carradine, Robert Altman, and Carolyn Pfeiffer.

Rueschmann, Eva. "Desire and Loss in Alan Rudolph's *The Moderns.*" *Literature/Film Quarterly* 22, no. 1 (1994): 57–61. Examines *The Moderns* in terms of the concept of male subjectivity and of the gaze as an articulation of desire. Interesting as one of the only psychoanalytical studies of Rudolph's work available to date.

Smith, Gavin. "Alan Rudolph: 'I Don't Have a Career, I Have a Careen.' " *Film Comment,* May–June 1993, 59–71. An extensive assessment of the director's work, covering all of his films. Offers particular insight into the making and meaning of *Equinox.* Also provides some discussion of

Rudolph's plans for the production of *Mrs. Parker and the Vicious Circle* (then called *Mrs. Parker and the Roundtable*).

Tanner, Louise. "Alan Rudolph." *Films in Review,* April 1990, 212–13. Brief and thoroughly superficial interview with the director at the time of the release of *Love at Large.* The article gives more insight into the writer than the subject.

Taylor, Paul. "Meet All the People—Alan Rudolph." *Monthly Film Bulletin,* November 1990, 340. Provides a brief biographical sketch and filmography. Largely made up of quotes from previous interviews with the director.

Trainor, Richard. "*The Moderns.*" *Sight and Sound,* Autumn 1988, 233–34. A discussion of the title film and an interview with Rudolph in which the director also discusses the critical reception of *Remember My Name,* his admiration for Altman, and the production of *Choose Me.*

FILMOGRAPHY

Premonition (also released as *The Impure*), 1970; released 1972
Production: Transvue Pictures Corporation/Joyce Productions
Executive Producer: Oscar Rudolph
Producer: Alan Rudolph
Co-producer: Christopher R. Robertson
Associate Producers: Al Overton, Jr., and Lee Harmon
Screenplay: Alan Rudolph
Photography: John Bailey
Photography Assistant: Jan Kiesser and John Graham
Special Effects Photography: Jan Kiesser
Editor: Richard Patterson
Assistant Editor: Carol Littleton
Music: Alex Del Zoppo, Tim Ray, and Tom Akers
Sound Recording: John Musselman
Cast: Carl Crow (Neil), Tim Ray (Andy), Winfrey Hestor Hill (Baker), Victor
    Izay (Professor Kilkenny), Judith Patterson (Janice), Michele Fitzsim-
    mons (Denise), Durt C. Lodd (John), Eddie Peterson (discothèque
    owner), Barry Brown (Mike), Miles Tilton (concert promoter), Doug
    Digioia (second discothèque owner), Cheryl Adams (Susan), Diana
    Daves (female student), John Holman (male student), Tom Akers (mem-
    ber of rock group), Alex Del Zoppo (member of rock group), Fred Her-
    rera (member of rock group), Andy Hare (member of rock group),
    Logan Williams (driver), Shelley Snell (inspector), Madelyn Gian-
    francesco (girl in dream), Toni Wager (girl in dream), Marguerite Wiley
    (girl in dream), Lee Alpert (fraternity brother), Joyce Rudolph (hippie at
    cabin), Larry Loveridge (hippie at cabin), Paul Katz (hippie at cabin)
Running Time: 80 minutes

Terror Circus (also released as *Barn of the Naked Dead* and *Nightmare Circus* [on video]), 1973
Production: CMC/Twin World Pictures
Producer: Gerald Cormier
Executive Producer: Shirlee F. Jamail
Screenplay: Roman Valenti
Story: Gerald Cormier

Photography: E. Lynn (Panavision; Technicolor)
Editing: M K Productions, Inc.
Art Direction: Bill Conway
Special Makeup and Visual Effects: Byrd Holland and Douglas White
Cast: Andrew Prine (André), Manuella Theiss (Simone), Sherry Alberoni (Sheri), Gyl Roland (Corrine), Sheila Bromley (Mrs. Baynes), Gil Lamb (Mr. Alvarez), Al Cormier (sheriff), Chuck Miles (Derek Moore), Jennifer Ashley (flower child), Laura Campbell (Laura)
Running Time: 86 minutes

Welcome to L.A., 1976

Production: United Artists; Lion's Gate Films
Producer: Robert Altman
Associate Producers: Robert Eggenweiler and Scott Bushnell
Production Executive: Tommy Thompson
Assistant Directors: Tommy Thompson and Tony Bishop
Screenplay: Alan Rudolph
Photography: Dave Myers (DeLuxe color)
Visual Consultant: J. Allen Highfill
Editors: William A. Sawyer and Tom Walls
Set Decorator: Dennis Parrish
Music/Songs: Richard Baskin
Costumes: Jules Melillo
Makeup: Monty Westmore
Sound Editor: David Horton
Cast: Keith Carradine (Carroll Barber), Sally Kellerman (Ann Goode), Geraldine Chaplin (Karen Hood), Harvey Keitel (Ken Hood), Lauren Hutton (Nona Bruce), Viveca Lindfors (Susan Moore), Sissy Spacek (Linda Murray), Denver Pyle (Carl Barber), John Considine (Jack Goode), Richard Baskin (Eric Wood), Allan Nicholls (Dana Howard), Cedric Scott (Faye), Mike Kaplan (Russell Linden), Diahann Abbott (Jeannette Ross)
Running Time: 106 minutes
Soundtrack recording: United Artists Records

Remember My Name, 1978

Production: Columbia; Lion's Gate
Producer: Robert Altman
Associate Producers: Scott Bushnell and Robert Eggenweiler
Production Executive: Tommy Thompson
Production Coordinator: Victoria Barney
Assistant Directors: Tommy Thompson, Peter Bergquist, and Bill Cosentino
Screenplay: Alan Rudolph
Photography: Tak Fujimoto (DeLuxe color)

Editors: Thomas Walls and William A. Sawyer
Songs: Alberta Hunter
Costumes: J. Allen Highfill
Makeup: Monty Westmore
Sound Editor: Sam Gemette
Cast: Geraldine Chaplin (Emily), Anthony Perkins (Neil Curry), Moses Gunn (Pike), Berry Berenson (Barbara Curry), Jeff Goldblum (Mr. Nudd), Timothy Thomerson (Jeff), Alfre Woodard (Rita), Marilyn Coleman (Teresa), Jeffrey S. Perry (Harry), Carlos Brown (Rusty), Dennis Franz (Franks), Terry Wills (waiter), Ina Gould (shopper), Jette Seear (saleslady), Belita Moreno (neighbor), Barbara Dodd (Barbara's mother), Jim Thalman (detective), Tom Oberhaus (policeman), Diana Daves (newscaster), Maysie Hoy (newscaster), Herb Kerns (newscaster), Steve Mendillo (newscaster), Richard Wahl (newscaster), George Walsh (newscaster)
Running Time: 94 minutes
Soundtrack Recording: Columbia

Roadie, 1980

Production: United Artists/Alive Enterprises/A Vivant Production
Producer: Carolyn Pfeiffer
Executive Producer: Zalman King
Screenplay: Big Boy Medlin and Michael Ventura
Story: Big Boy Medlin, Michael Ventura, Zalman King, and Alan Rudolph
Photography: David Myers (Technicolor)
Editor: Tom Walls
Supervising Editor: Carol Littleton
Production Designer: Paul Peters
Set Decoration: Richard Friedman
Costumes: Jered Edd Green and Gail Bixby
Music: Craig Hundley
Sound: Richard Goodman (Dolby stereo)
Sound Editors: William L. Manger, Richard Oswald, Jim Bullock, and Joanne D'Antonio
Cast: Meat Loaf (Travis W. Redfish), Kaki Hunter (Lola Bouilliabase), Art Carney (Corpus C. Redfish), Gailard Sartain (B. B. Muldoon), Don Cornelius (Mohammed Johnson), Rhonda Bates (Alice Poo), Joe Spano (Ace), Richard Marion (George), Sonny Davis (Bird), Hamilton Camp (Grady), Ginger Varney (weather girl), Alice Cooper, Alvin Crow and the Pleasant Valley Boys, Asleep at the Wheel, Blondie, Roy Orbison, Hank Williams, Jr.
Running Time: 106 minutes
Soundtrack Recording: Warner Brothers Records

Endangered Species, 1982

Production: MGM/UA Entertainment; Alive Enterprises
Producer: Carolyn Pfeiffer
Executive Producer: Zalman King
Screenplay: Alan Rudolph and John Binder
Story: Judson Klinger and Richard Woods
Photography: Paul Lohmann (Panavision; Metrocolor)
Editor: Tom Walls
Production Design: Trevor Williams
Set Design: Eric Orbom
Set Decoration: R. Chris Westlund
Special Effects: Jonnie Burke and Steve Galic
Costumes: Betsy Cox
Music: Gary Wright
Sound: Jim Tanenbaum
Cast: Robert Urich (Ruben Castle), JoBeth Williams (Harriet Purdue), Paul
    Dooley (Joe Hiatt), Hoyt Axton (Ben Morgan), Marin Kanter (Macken-
    zie Castle), Peter Coyote (Steele), Gailard Sartain (mayor), Dan Hedaya
    (Peck), Harry Carey, Jr. (Dr. Emmer), John Considine (Burnside),
    Margery Bond (Judy Hiatt), Joseph G. Medalis (lawyer), Patrick Houser
    (Chester), Alvin Crow (Deputy Wayne), Ned Dowd (Deputy Bobby),
    Kent Rizley (Deputy Ray), Heather Menzies (Susan), Michelle Davison
    (Mrs. Haskins), Henry G. Sanders (Dr. Ross), Vernon Weddle (Varney)
Running Time: 97 minutes

Return Engagement, 1983

Production: Island Pictures; Alive Enterprises
Producer: Carolyn Pfeiffer
Associate Producer: Barbara Leary
Assistant Director: Bruce Chevillat
Photography: Jan Kiesser (Foto-Kem Industries Color; 16mm)
Editor: Tom Walls
Music: Adrian Belew
Sound: Douglas Vaughn
Cast: G. Gordon Liddy, Timothy Leary, Carole Hemingway
Running Time: 89 minutes

Choose Me, 1984

Production: Island Alive
Producers: Carolyn Pfeiffer and David Blocker
Executive Producers: Shep Gordon and Chris Blackwell
Screenplay: Alan Rudolph
Photography: Jan Kiesser (Movielab color)
Editing: Mia Goldman

Production Design: Steven Legler
Costumes: Tracy Tynan
Makeup: Ed Ternes
Songs: Teddy Pendergrass
Sound: Ron Judkins, Robert Jackson
Sound Editor: Dody Dorn, Robert Grieve
Cast: Keith Carradine (Mickey Bolton), Lesley Ann Warren (Eve), Genevieve Bujold (Dr. Nancy Love/Anne), Patrick Bauchau (Zack Antoine), Rae Dawn Chong (Pearl Antoine), John Larroquette (Billy Ace), Edward Ruscha (Ralph Chomsky), Gailard Sartain (Mueller), Robert Gould (Lou), John Considine (Dr. Ernest Greene, voice), Jodi Buss (Babs), Sandra Will (Ida), Mike E. Kaplan (Harve), Russell Parr (Bradshaw), Teresa Velarde (studio secretary), Henry G. Sanders (hospital administrator), Margery Bond (cousin), Debra Dusay (Nurse La Mer), Minnie Lindsay (woman on bus), Richard Marion (Gilda), Albert Stanislaus (Max), Karyn Isaacs (Farrah), Elizabeth Lloyd Shaw (Miss Muffin), Edward C. Lawson (Chrome), Chase Holiday (Champagne), Patrick McFadden (Rudy)
Running Time: 108 minutes

Songwriter, 1985

Production: Tri-Star Pictures
Producer: Sydney Pollack
Executive Producer: Mike Moder
Screenplay: Bud Shrake
Photography: Matthew Leonetti (Metrocolor)
Editing: Stuart Pappé
Production Design: Joel Schiller
Set Decoration: Barbara Krieger
Costumes: Ernest Misko and Kathleen Gore-Misko
Makeup: Edward Ternes and Greg LaCava
Music: Larry Cansler
Songs: Willie Nelson and Kris Kristofferson
Music Editor: George A. Martin
Sound: Arthur Rochester (Dolby stereo)
Sound Editors: Robert Grieve, Patrick Drumond, Dennis Drummond, George Anderson, Dody Dorn, John Hoeren, and Reid Paul Martin
Cast: Willie Nelson (Doc Jenkins), Kris Kristofferson (Blackie Buck), Lesley Ann Warren (Gilda), Rip Torn (Dino McLeish), Melinda Dillon (Honey Carder), Mickey Raphael (Arly), Rhonda Dotson (Corkie), Richard C. Sarafian (Rodeo Rocky), Robert Gould (Ralph), Sage Parker (Pattie McLeish), Shannon Wilcox (Anita), Jeff MacKay (Hogan), Gailard Sartain (Mulreaux), Stephen Bruton (Sam), Glen Clark (Paul), Cleve Dupin (Road Manager), B. C. Cooper (Cooper), Poodie Locke (Purvis), Joe

Keyes (Eddie), Amanda Bishop (daughter number 1), Kristin Renfro (daughter number 2), Sammy Allred (disc jockey), Bill Boyd (Blind Tommy's brother), Steve Fromholtz (engineer), Johnny Gimble (fiddle player), Eloise Schmitt (girl on bus), Kate Cadenhead (groupie), Christi Carafano (girl in bed), Joe Gallien (electronics engineer), Gates Moore (first concert hall manager), Larry Gorham (concert hall manager), Jackie King (guitar player), Catherine Molloy (Doc's girlfriend), Bobby Rambo (party guest), Michael Reesberg (Roarer roadie), John Shaw (cashier), Pete Stauber (vacuum cleaner salesman), Larry Trader (golf roadie), Priscilla Dougherty (incredulous woman)
Running Time: 94 minutes
Soundtrack Recording: Columbia

Trouble in Mind, 1986

Production: Island Alive/Terry Glinwood/Alive Films
Producers: Carolyn Pfeiffer and David Blocker
Executive Producer: Cary Brokaw
Screenplay: Alan Rudolph
Photography: Toyomichi Kurita (CFI color)
Editing: Tom Walls and Sally Coryn Allen
Production Design: Steven Legler
Set Designer: Don Ferguson
Special Effects: Bob Burns
Costumes: Tracy Tynan
Makeup: Edward Ternes
Stunt Coordinator: Greg Walker
Music: Mark Isham
Sound: Ron Judkins and Robert Jackson
Sound Editor: Dody Dorn
Cast: Kris Kristofferson (Hawk [John Hawkins]), Keith Carradine (Coop), Lori Singer (Georgia), Genevieve Bujold (Wanda), Joe Morton (Solo), Divine (Hilly Blue), George Kirby (Lieutenant Gunther), John Considine (Nate Nathanson), Dirk Blocker (Rambo), Albert Hall (Leo), Gailard Sartain (Fat Adolph), Robert Gould (Mardy Skoog), Antonia Dauphin (Sonja Nathanson), Billy Silva (Elmo), Caitlin Ferguson (Spike), Allen Nicholls (Sector Representative Pete Regis), Debray Dusay (Marie La Mer), Elizabeth Kaye (Bunny), Rick Tutor (Bill), Joanne Klein (Eve Lamour), Jill Klein (Nancy Lamour), William Hall (long militiaman), David Klein (short militiaman), Andrea Stein (Maria), David McIntyre (McBride), Steve Danton (Steve Zarque), Mara Scott-Wood (Trixie), Robert Kim (Chiene), Robert Lee (Ho), Matt Almond (Slick), Tracy Kristofferson (Tammy Regis), Ron Ben Jarrett (Bouncer), William Earl Ray (long prison guard), Steven Ross (short prison guard), Patricia Tyler (soldier), Toni Cross (bartender), Sarah Yvonne Murray

(Samaritan), Carl Sander (wealthy man), Judy Lynn Gratton (wealthy woman), Stuart Manne (Little Caesar), B. J. Alexander (Snookums), Danielle Aubuchon (Shana), Nanci Anton (Eva), Barry Press (salesman), J. Morgan Armstrong (Mo), Frank Gargani (Ginny), Felix Casares (Scholar), David Quintera (Blackie), R. Fox (Officer Clark), M. James Clark (Officer Fox), James Etue (Shamus), Francis Diamond (Diamond), Patti Dobrowolski (Vega), Pamela Gray (Dot), Lee Ann Fuji (Rose), Jabus Wesson (Jingles), J. R. Smith (Pud), James Fulgium (Flip), Terry Morgan (pimp), James Crabtree (fireman), Tammy Wolfe (tour guide), Stephen Sneed (bellboy)

Running Time: 111 minutes

Soundtrack Recording: Island Records

Made in Heaven, 1987

Production: Lorimer Motion Pictures

Producers: Raynold Gideon, Bruce A. Evans, and David Blocker

Screenplay: Bruce A. Evans and Raynold Gideon

Photography: Jan Kiesser (Panavision; Metrocolor; Technicolor; Duart)

Editing: Tom Walls

Production Design: Paul Peters

Art Direction: Steven Legler

Set Designers: David Boatwright and Gershon Ginsburg

Costumes: April Ferry

Makeup: Edward Ternes and Annie Menassian

Special Effects: Max W. Anderson

Music: Mark Isham

Sound: Ron Judkins, Robert Jackson

Sound Editor: Dody Dorn

Stunt Coordinator: Greg Walker

Cast: Timothy Hutton (Mike Shea/Elmo Barnett), Kelly McGillis (Annie Packert/Allyson Chandler), Maureen Stapleton (Aunt Lisa), Ann Wedgeworth (Annette Shea), James Gammon (Steve Shea), Mare Winningham (Brenda Carlucci), Don Murray (Ben Chandler), Timothy Daly (Tom Donnelly), David Rasche (Donald Sumner), Amanda Plummer (Wiley Foxx), Willard Pugh (Guy Blanchard/Brian Dutton), Vyto Ruginis (Lyman McCray), Neil Young (truck driver), Tom Petty (Stanky), Ric Ocasek (Shank), Marj Dusay (Mrs. Packert), Ray Gideon (Mr. Packert), Zack Finch (Billy Packert), Rob Knepper (Orrin), James Tolkan (Mr. Bjornstead), Gailard Sartain (Sam Morrell), John Considine (angel), Elliott Rabinowitz (Woody, talent coordinator), Tom Robbins (Mario the toymaker), Debra Dusay (Miss Barnett), Patricia Earnest (Mrs. Burwell), Leon Martell (Reginald/TV interviewer), Dave Michaels and Billy Jo Rucker (TV interviewers), Paul Sloan (Young Elmo), Larry Sloan (Uncle Gus), Lauren Hill (Young Ally), Ann Owens

(Grandmother Chandler), Tom Walls (C. C. Stank), Elliot Street (Andy), Michael Klastorin (Murray), Robert Gould and Chester Clark (Chandler Toy Co. executives), Meegan Lee Ochs (Ally's assistant), Henry Sanders (Henry), Dirk Blocker (Shorty), Ellen Barkin (Lucille—uncredited), Debra Winger (Emmett Humbird—uncredited [Emmett credited as being played by himself])
Running Time: 103 minutes
Soundtrack Recording: Elektra/Asylum Records

The Moderns, 1988

Production: Nelson Entertainment; Alive Films; Pfeiffer/Blocker Production
Producers: Carolyn Pfeiffer and David Blocker
Executive Producer: Shep Gordon
Screenplay: Alan Rudolph and Jon Bradshaw
Photography: Toyomichi Kurita (CFI color)
Additional Photography: Jan Kiesser
Editing: Debra T. Smith and Scott Brock
Production Design: Steven Legler
Set Decoration: Jean-Baptiste Tard
Special Effects: Jacques Godbout
Costumes: Renée April
Makeup: Micheline Trepanier and Diane Simard
Stunt Cordinator: Greg Walker
Music: Mark Isham
Sound: Ron Judkins and Robert Jackson (Dolby stereo)
Sound Editors: Dody Dorn and Blake Leyh
Cast: Keith Carradine (Nick Hart), Linda Fiorentino (Rachel Stone), John Lone (Bertram Stone), Wallace Shawn (Oiseau), Genevieve Bujold (Libby Valentin), Geraldine Chaplin (Nathalie de Ville), Kevin J. O'Connor (Ernest Hemingway), CharlElie Couture (L'Evidence), Elsa Raven (Gertrude Stein), Ali Giron (Alice B. Toklas), Michael Rudder (Buffy), Paul Buissoneau (Alexandre), Lenie Scofie (femme de lettres), Reynald Bouchard (Chapelle), Flora Balzano (Pia Delarue), Beverly Murray (Eve), Renee Lee (chanteuse), Gailard Sartain (New York critic), David Stein and Hubert Loiselle (art critics), Marthe Turgeon (Rose Selavy), Charlie Biddle (Charlie the bass player), Glen Bradley (saxophonist), Didier Hoffman (priest), Jean-Jacques Desjardins (Hart's concierge), Ada Fuoco (herself), Harry Hill (Mr. Brown), Marcel Girard (Nathalie's chauffeur), Danielle Schneider and Stephanie Biddle (filles de nuit), Louis Pharand (referee), Daniel Bloch (M. Raymond), Julien Carletti (Café Moderne waiter), Michael Wilson (surrealist poet), Robert Gould (Blackie), Antonia Dauphin (Babette), Veronique Bellegarde (Laurette), Isabelle Serra (Armand), Meegan Lee Ochs (Francis), Brooke Smith (Abigail), Pierre Chagnon (Stone's first bodyguard), Eric Gaudry

(Stone's first bodyguard), Timothy Webber (Stone's business associate), Mance Edmond (Coco), Norman Brathwaite (Butler Laloux)
Running Time: 126 minutes
Soundtrack Recording: Virgin Movie Music

Love at Large, 1990
Production: Orion
Producer: David Blocker
Associate Producer: Stuart Besser
Production Executive: Dana Mayer
Production Coordinator: Janice Reynolds
Assistant Directors: Jerry Ziesmer and Michael McCloud-Thompson
Screenplay: Alan Rudolph
Photography: Elliot Davis (DeLuxe color)
Additional Photography: James Glennon
Editor: Lisa Churgin
Production Designer: Steven Legler
Special Effects: Frank Ceglia
Music: Mark Isham
Costume Designer: Ingrid Ferrin
Makeup: Cynthia Barr
Supervising Sound Editor: Richard King
Cast: Tom Berenger (Harry Dobbs), Elizabeth Perkins (Stella Wynkowski), Anne Archer (Miss Dolan), Kate Capshaw (Ellen McGraw), Annette O'Toole (Mrs. King), Ted Levine (Frederick King/James McGraw), Ann Magnuson (Doris), Kevin J. O'Connor (Art), Ruby Dee (Corrine Dart), Barry Miller (Marty), Neil Young (Rick), Meegan Lee Ochs (bellhop), Gailard Sartain (taxi driver), Robert Gould (tavern bartender), Dirk Blocker (Hiram Culver), Bob Terhune (Harley), Ariana Lamon-Anderson (Missy McGraw), Michael Wilson (Blue Danube maître d'), Debra Dusay (Blue Danube waitress)
Running Time: 97 minutes
Soundtrack Recording: Virgin Movie Music

Mortal Thoughts, 1991
Production: Columbia Pictures; New Visions Entertainment/Polar Entertainment Corporation; Rufglen Films
Producer: John Fiedler, Mark Tarlov
Executive Producers: Taylor Hackford and Stuart Benjamin
Screenplay: William Reilly and Claude Kerven
Photography: Elliot Davis
Editor: Tom Walls
Production Designer: Howard Cummings
Art Director: Robert K. Shaw, Jr.

Set Decorator: Beth Kushnick
Costumes: Hope Hanafin
Makeup: Janet Flora, Joseph A. Campayno, and Scott Eddo
Music: Mark Isham
Sound: Gary Alper and Steven Krause
Sound Editor: Richard King
Stunt Coordinator: Greg Walker
Cast: Demi Moore (Cynthia Kellogg), Glenne Headly (Joyce Urbanski), Bruce Willis (James Urbanski), John Pankow (Arthur Kellogg), Harvey Keitel (Detective John Wood), Billie Neal (Linda Nealon), Frank Vincent (Dominic Marino), Karen Shallo (Gloria Urbanski), Crystal Field (Jeanette Marino), Maryanne Leone (Aunt Rita), Marc Tantillo (usher), Doris McCarthy (Pat, Cynthia's mother), Christopher Scotellaro (Joey Urbanski), Ron J. Amodea (band leader), Leonid Merzon (Yuri), Kelly Cinnante (Cookie), Christopher Peacock (Irish kid number 2), Bruce Smolanoff (Irish kid number 3), Elain Graham (woman police sergeant), Thomas Quinn (Detective Seltzer), Brandon Messemer, Richard Messemer (Cynthia's baby), Larry Attile (Sydney Levitt), Roger Shamas (Krishna Kolhatkar), Star Jasper (Lauren), Lindsay Rodio (Jennifer Kellogg, age three), Julie Garfield (Maria Urbanski), Edward Chip Rogers (detective), David A. Willis (Mr. Urbanski), James Pecora (cop), Elaine Eldridge (customer in salon), Kimberly Comprix (Tina), Anna Marie Wieder (Candy)
Running Time: 102 minutes

Equinox, 1993

Production: S. C. Entertainment International
Producer: David Blocker
Executive Producers: Nicolas Stiliadis, Syd Cappe, and Sandy Stern
Screenplay: Alan Rudolph
Photography: Elliot Davis (Panavision)
Editor: Michael Ruscio
Production Designer: Steven Legler
Art Director: Randy Eriksen
Set Decorator: Cliff Cunningham
Costume Design: Sharen Davis
Key Makeup: Kathryn Bihr
Supervising Sound Editor: John Nutt
Stunt Coordinator: Greg Walker
Cast: Matthew Modine (Henry Petosa/Freddy Ace/Immanuel), Lara Flynn Boyle (Beverly Franks), Fred Ward (Mr. Paris), Tyra Ferrell (Sonya Kirk), Marisa Tomei (Rosie Rivers), Kevin J. O'Connor (Russell Franks), Tate Donovan (Richie Nunn), Lori Singer (Sharon Ace), M. Emmett Walsh (Pete Petosa), Gailard Sartain (Dandridge), Tony Genaro (Eddie Gutier-

rez), Angel Aviles (Anna Gutierrez), Dirk Blocker (Red), Kirsten Ellickson (Young Helena), Pat Clemons (Helena), Debra Dusay (Judith Hammer), Les Podewell (Jerome Hammer), Meegan Lee Ochs (Bess), Carlos Sanz (Harold), Lenora Finley (Maye), Isabell Monk (apartment superintendent), Billy Silva (Sabujii), Tom Kasat (I. M. Strong), Diane Wheeler-Nicholson (self-defense victim/drunk woman), Paul Meshejian (Ralph), Robert Gould (Mel), Shirley Venard (Villa Capri waitress), Willis Burks II (Willie), Pancho Demmings (morgue worker), Jack Walsh (newspaper man), Martin Marinaro (attendant), Elizabeth Ann Gray (large woman on bus), Wayne A. Evenson (large woman's companion), Randy Gust (bus punk), Matthew Dudley and John Sargent (toughs), Frank Davis (Marsh), Mark Modine (cook), Ken Earl (banker), Vinnie Curto (gangster), Chris George (Villa Capri pianist), Kerry Hoyt (Kerry), Rebecca Sabot (Paris's girlfriend), Suzette Tarzia (Charlene)
Running Time: 110 minutes
Soundtrack Recording: Varese Sarabande

Mrs. Parker and the Vicious Circle, 1994

Production: Fine Line Features
Producer: Robert Altman
Executive Producers: Scott Bushnell and Ira Deutchman
Co-Producer/First Assistant Director: Allan Nicholls
Screenplay: Alan Rudolph and Randy Sue Coburn
Photography: Jan Kiesser
Editor: Suzy Elmiger
Music: Mark Isham
Production Designer: Francois Seguin
Costume Designers: John Hay and Renée April
Cast: Jennifer Jason Leigh (Dorothy Parker), Campbell Scott (Robert Benchley), Matthew Broderick (Charles MacArthur), Andrew McCarthy (Eddie Parker), Peter Gallagher (Alan Campbell), Jennifer Beals (Gertrude Benchley), Gwyneth Paltrow (Paula Hunt), Sam Robards (Harold Ross), Martha Plimpton (Jane Grant), Tom McGowan (Alexander Woolcott), Stephen Baldwin (Roger Spaulding), Wallace Shawn (Horatio Byrd), Lili Taylor (Edna Ferber), James LeGros (Deems Taylor), Keith Carradine (Will Rogers), Nick Cassavetes (Robert Sherwood), Jane Adams (Ruth Hale), Gary Basaraba (Heywood Broun), Rebecca Miller (Neysa McMein), David Thornton (George S. Kaufman), Matt Malloy (Marc Connelly), Peter Benchley (Frank Crowninshield), Mina Badie (Joanie Gerard), Amelia Campbell (Mary Brandon Sherwood), Jon Favreau (Elmer Rice), Gabriel Gascon (Georges Attends), Malcolm Gets (F. Scott Fitzgerald), David Gow (Donald Ogden Stewart), Heather Graham (Marry Kennedy Taylor), Jean-Michael Henry (Harpo Marx),

Jake Johannsen (John Peter Toohey), Randy Lowell (Alvan Barach),
Leni Parker (Beatrice Kaufman), Chip Zien (Franklin P. Adams)
Running Time: 127 minutes
Soundtrack Recording: Varese Sarabande

INDEX

Numbers in italics refer to photographs.

THE AUTHOR

Richard Ness is an instructor in the Department of Communication at Wayne State University and has taught film history, theory, and criticism at Iowa State University and the Octagon Center for the Arts. His articles and essays have been published in *The International Dictionary of Films and Filmmakers*, the *Hitchcock Annual*, and the *Des Moines Register*. Ness received an M.S. in mass communications and a B.A. in telecommunicative arts from Iowa State. He is the author of *From Headline Hunter to Superman: A Journalism Filmography*, and for his work on the topic he received a Research Excellence Award from Iowa State. His film production work includes acting as production manager for the documentary *Strengths and Weaknesses: College Students with Learning Disabilities* and serving as faculty advisor for the award-winning student film *The Jean Seberg Story*.

THE EDITOR

Frank E. Beaver was born in Cleveland, North Carolina, in 1938 and received his B.A. and M.A. at the University of North Carolina, Chapel Hill, and his Ph.D. at the University of Michigan, where he chairs the Department of Communication. He is the author of *Oliver Stone: Wakeup Cinema* (also in this series), Twayne's *Dictionary of Film Terms,* and three books on the art and history of the motion picture. For 20 years he has served as media commentator for National Public Radio stations WUOM-WVGR-WFUM.